THE HUMAN Race

SEAN CALLERY
DONOUGH O'MALLEY

QED

CONTENTS

FASTER, HIGHER, FURTHER — 4

- **RUN!** The race to sprint — 6
- **MICHAEL PHELPS** The race to swim — 8
- **THROW!** The race to fling further — 10
- **THE OLYMPICS** The biggest sporting event in the world — 12
- **PARALYMPICS** The race without limits — 14
- **RIDE!** The race to pedal — 16
- **DRIVE!** The race on four wheels — 18
- **SNOW!** The race to slide — 20

JOURNEYS AND EXPEDITIONS — 22

- **TRADE!** The race to link east and west — 24
- **CHRISTOPHER COLUMBUS** The race across the Atlantic — 26
- **SAIL!** The race around the world — 28
- **ELLEN MACARTHUR** The solo race — 30
- **THE UNDERWORLD** The race to the bottom of the sea — 32
- **DAVID LIVINGSTONE** The race across Africa — 34
- **HEAT!** The race across Australia — 36
- **AMUNDSEN VS. SCOTT** The race to the South Pole — 38
- **AMELIA EARHART** The race across the sky — 40
- **NORGAY & HILLARY** The race to the top — 42

TRANSPORT AND VEHICLES — 44

- **SHIPS** The race to sail — 46
- **CARS** The race on four wheels — 48
- **BIKES** The race on two wheels — 50
- **TRAINS** The rolling story — 52
- **BALLOONS** The race into the sky — 54
- **WRIGHT BROTHERS** The race to fly — 56
- **ROCKETS** The race to space — 58
- **APOLLO 11** The race to the moon — 60

SCIENCE AND OUR WORLD — 62

- **STAYING ALIVE!** The race against disease — 64
- **CHARLES DARWIN** The race to evolve — 66
- **FIX ME!** The race to cure — 68
- **THE BODY** The race to see inside — 70
- **MARIE CURIE** The radiation race — 72
- **LOOKING UP** The race to know the stars — 74
- **ISAAC NEWTON** The race to understand gravity — 76

TECHNOLOGY — 78

- **THE SPARK** The race for electricity — 80
- **WHEELS** A turning point — 82
- **COMPUTERS** The data race — 84
- **POWER!** The race for energy — 86
- **COMMUNICATION** From smoke signals to SMS — 88
- **MEDIA** The race to be entertained — 90
- **FARMING** The race to grow food — 92
- **FOOD** The race to eat better — 94

INDEX — 96

INTRODUCTION

One thing that makes humans special is our imagination: we wonder what will happen if we try something new. This is the spark that encourages us to run faster, explore further, investigate mysteries and try out new ideas as we compete in the human race.

Fire first

Maybe our greatest early achievement was to light a fire and keep it going. The flames helped keep us warm, warned away unwelcome animals and cooked the ones we caught!

Since then we have explored our planet and the worlds beyond it and investigated our bodies to understand how they work. On the way we have pushed our bodies to their limits, whether sailing rough seas, figuring out tricky problems or trying to throw a stone further than a friend.

What have sheep got to do with tennis?

We have made countless discoveries and inventions throughout history. These usually follow on from something already known, building on our knowledge and skills. For example, a machine with rotating blades that made woollen cloth smooth gave Edwin Budding the idea for the lawnmower in 1830. Once people could cut their grass short, they played outdoor games on it and invented tennis. Then we improved the wooden racquets with graphite and fibreglass... As this book shows, one idea leads to another, and another...

4

FASTER HIGHER FURTHER

Humans love to race! We enjoy competition and we like to win. Find out who runs the fastest, who's the speediest swimmer and how humans can zoom rapidly, on two wheels or four...

FASTER, HIGHER, FURTHER

RUN! THE RACE TO SPRINT

People have always raced: to hunt or escape animals, because they are in a hurry to get somewhere, or to keep fit. Years ago, when soldiers marched and fought on foot, tough running races were part of army training, and this continues to this day.

Who's the fastest?

The 100-metre sprint is the fastest race in the world. The champion is Jamaican athlete Usain Bolt who ran it in 9.58 seconds at the World Championships in Berlin, in 2009. The fastest woman is American athlete Florence Griffith-Joyner who ran 100 metres in 10.49 seconds. Irish athlete Jason Smyth is the fastest paralympic sprinter in the world. He is visually impaired (which means it is difficult for him to see clearly) and has the 100-metre record time of 10.46 seconds.

Different races

Athletes run fast in lots of ways. Shorter races are called sprints. Middle distance races are from 800 to 3,000 metres, and running further than that is called long distance. Other running races are:

- **RELAYS** – teams (usually of four) pass a stick called a baton to the next runner
- **HURDLES** – competitors jump over obstacles called hurdles
- **STEEPLECHASE** – a race with hurdles and water jumps
- **RACE WALKING** – one foot must always be touching the ground during the race

USAIN BOLT won 20 Olympic and world championship gold medals in 21 events between 2008 and 2016.

6

The longest

The longest race is the marathon, run along streets for 42.195 kilometres. Its history goes back thousands of years to Ancient Greece. Kenyan Eliud Kipchoge made history as the first person to run a marathon in under two hours.

The 4-minute mile

It was a big moment when Roger Bannister broke the 'four-minute mile' barrier, running the distance in three minutes 59.4 seconds in 1954.

Are we getting faster?

Maybe not. Tracks of humans from 20,000 years ago show they ran at 37 kilometres per hour in bare feet on soft mud. They had to be fast to catch or escape wild animals. Usain Bolt's 9.69-second 100-metre run was at 42 kilometres per hour, in running shoes with gripping spikes on a special running track. Athletes run much faster on rubber or synthetic tracks than on cinder or grass.

MARLOU VAN RHIJN is the fastest female sprinter on artifical limbs.

ROGER BANNISTER was very proud of his record-breaking race, but considered his later achievements in his medical career to be more significant.

How to be the fastest

Today's top athletes work full-time to be the quickest.

- They wear lightweight shoes and clothes.
- They work on things like how long to stride, how to pump their arms and elbows, the best way to push off with their toes and feet and the best way to land their feet.
- They eat healthy fresh food and take extra vitamins.
- They visit the gym to build body strength.

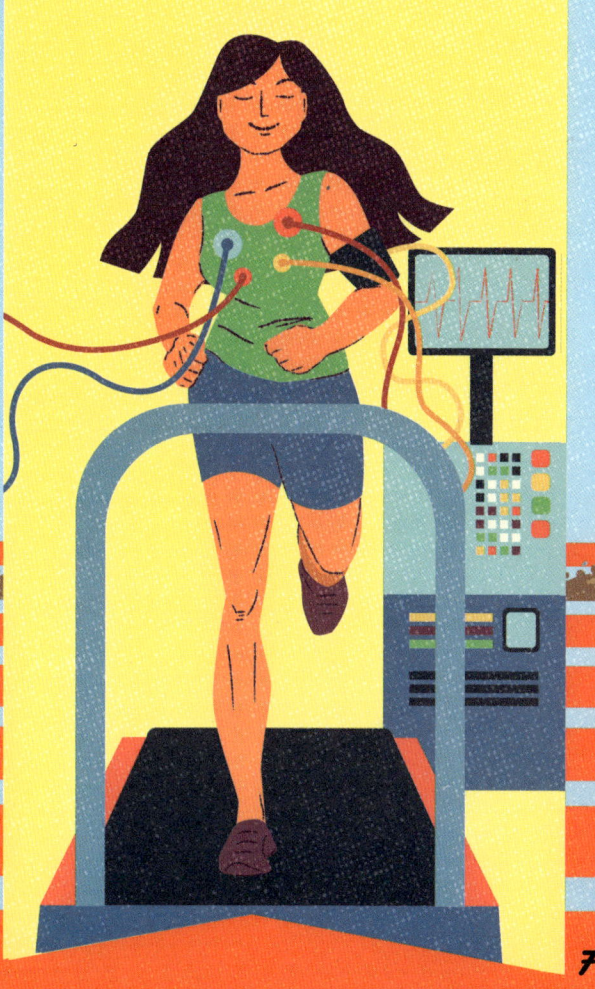

FASTER, HIGHER, FURTHER

MICHAEL PHELPS THE RACE TO SWIM

Michael Phelps is the most successful swimmer ever, and one of the greatest athletes of all time. He was born in 1985 in Baltimore, Maryland, USA. Michael is built for swimming. He grew to 1.93 metres tall, has long arms and big feet to power him through the water, a stocky chest and relatively short legs to help him glide smoothly. Some children made fun of his long arms and thin body when he was young.

While he was naturally suited to swimming, he also worked very hard. He trained for hours every day and took part in his first Olympics when he was just 15. In 2008, he set a record by winning eight gold medals in one Olympics. By the end of his career he had won 28 Olympic medals, including 23 golds. This is far more than any other athlete.

The Medley
One of Michael's best events was the 4x100-metre medley, a tough race where competitors swim 100 metres in four different styles.

Front crawl
This is the fastest technique, and is probably very old, but it was first described in 1844 after two Native American swimmers surprised watchers with it at a competition in England. Circle your arms forwards one after the other and kick your feet up and down.

FRONT CRAWL SPRINT

England to France

Michael swam in the pool, but some swimmers prefer the open sea. One of the greatest challenges is to swim the English Channel between England and France. The channel is 33.8 kilometres across, but tides and currents mean swimmers cover much more than this. The first man to do it was Captain Matthew Webb in 1875, and the first woman was Gertrude Ederle in 1926.

GERTRUDE EDERLE

Backstroke
Lie on your back, arms rotating, legs kicking. It is an ancient technique but officially dates from 1904.

Breaststroke
On your front, sweep your arms forwards and back while doing a 'frog kick'. Stone Age cave paintings show this style being used.

Butterfly
Move both your arms up, over, forwards and back together while your legs do the 'butterfly' or 'dolphin' kick at the same time. It developed from the front crawl.

9

FASTER, HIGHER, FURTHER

THROW! THE RACE TO FLING FURTHER

Throwing needs good hand and eye co-ordination, plus the ability to grip well and a strong arm to launch. Early humans found this a valuable skill, from lobbing wood into fires to chucking rocks to hunt or fight. The skill is also used in many sports and games.

	ORIGINS	WHAT IS THROWN?	HOW?
DISCUS	Dates back to 708BC. Competitors throw a flat disk. The first were stone, then metal.	Today the discus is plastic with a metal rim. It weighs 2 kilograms for men, 1 kilogram for women.	Spin in a circle before launching the discus as far as you can.
JAVELIN	Developed from spears used to hunt and fight in ancient times. They reached the Olympics in 1908.	A metal-tipped javelin. Men's are 2.6-2.7 metres long and weigh at least 800 grams. Women's are 2.2-2.3 metres and weigh 600 grams.	Run and launch without crossing the 'foul line'. The javelin must land tip first.
SHOT PUT	Developed after cannonballs were invented in the thirteenth century. It was an Olympic sport from 1896.	A metal ball. It weighs 7.26 kilograms for men, and 4 kilograms for women.	Spin in a circle before launching the shotput as far as you can.
HAMMER	It started with tools that blacksmiths used to shape metal. Throwing them was a sport in Scotland from the 15th century. It entered the Olympics in 1900.	A metal ball on the end of a steel wire attached to a handle. It weighs 7.26 kilograms for men, 4 kilograms for women.	Spin the hammer above your head while turning inside a circle up to four times before letting go.

WOMEN'S RECORD

76.8 metres by
Gabriele Reinsch, 1988.

72.28 metres by
Barbora Špotáková, 2008.

22.63 metres by
Natalya Lisovskaya, 1987.

82.98 metres by
Anita Włodarczyk, 2016.

MEN'S RECORD

74.08 metres by
Jürgen Schult, 1986.

98.48 metres by
Jan Železný, 1996.

23.12 metres by
Randy Barnes, 1990.

86.74 metres by
Yuriy Sedykh, 1986.

Throwing sports

Some sports that use throwing techniques are:

BOWLS Wooden balls are thrown at a target. One of the oldest bowls clubs is in Southampton, England, dating from 1299.

DARTS Arrows are thrown at a board. This is an ancient game but the modern version dates from 1896.

BASKETBALL A team game where the ball is bounced and thrown to others or into a high net, first played in 1891.

And there are sports where an opponent uses a bat to hit a thrown ball:

CRICKET A bowler launches a leather ball towards a batter guarding wooden stumps. The fastest bowl ever was 161.26 kilometres per hour by Shoaib Akhtar, 2003.

BASEBALL A throwing, hitting and running game. The fastest 'pitch' at a batter was 169.14 kilometres per hour by Aroldis Chapman, 2010.

Throwing better

The whole of the body is needed for a powerful ball throw: stand side on, pointing at the target, lean back and then shift your weight to lean forwards as you drop the pointing arm and whip your throwing arm over your shoulder, snapping the wrist forwards just as you release the ball.

FASTER, HIGHER, FURTHER

776 BC
The first known Olympic games was a religious festival where the main event was an animal sacrifice to the god Zeus. Only men competed and there was just one race: a 192-metre run. The event was repeated every four years and new sports were introduced such as wrestling, jumping, chariot racing and horse-riding. Winners won a wreath of leaves.

1896
The games were revived in Athens, Greece. 14 countries competed in 43 events.

1904
From now on winners won gold, silver or bronze medals.

1924
The first winter Olympics took place in Chamonix, France.

1936
Jesse Owens, an African American athlete, won gold in the 100 metres, 200 metres, long jump and 4x100-metre relay in Berlin.

THE OLYMPICS
The biggest sporting event in the world

396 BC
The last Olympic games in ancient Greece took place.

1900
Women joined for the first time: 11 women competed in either tennis or golf.

1913
The image of five linked rings was designed. The rings represent five continents (not including Antarctica and including the Americas as one). The colours chosen were black, blue, red, yellow and green. Every national flag has at least one of these colours.

1928
The Olympic flame was lit for the first time in Amsterdam, Netherlands (it still burns at today's Olympics). Women competed in track and field events for the first time.

1952
Czech runner Emil Zátopek was the only person ever to win the 5,000 metres, 10,000 metres, and marathon events in the same Olympiad, in Helsinki.

1984

In the winter event, British ice dancers Jayne Torvill and Christopher Dean got perfect scores from every judge, as well as the gold medal. Skier Marja-Liisa Kirvesniemi-Hämäläinen of Finland became the only woman to compete in six different Olympics.

2000

In Sydney, Australia, British rower Steven Redgrave became the first in his sport to win gold medals in five consecutive Olympics.

1994

The winter Olympics was held after two years to start a separate four-year cycle.

2012

Britain's Mo Farah became a national hero by winning the 5,000 and 10,000 metres races in London.

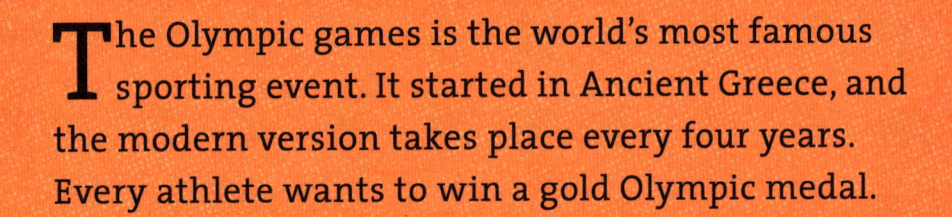

The Olympic games is the world's most famous sporting event. It started in Ancient Greece, and the modern version takes place every four years. Every athlete wants to win a gold Olympic medal.

1988

East German Christa Rothenburger won a speed skating gold in the winter games plus a cycling silver in the summer event to become the first person to win medals in both Olympiads in the same year.

2008

Jamaican sprinter Usain Bolt (see page 6) broke the world and Olympic records in both the 100 metres and 200 metres events. He also set a new record in the 100 metre team relay. Michael Phelps won a record eight gold medals in a single Olympics (see page 8).

1976

Gymnast Nadia Comăneci earned seven 'perfect 10' scores – no one had achieved even one before.

1988

At the Calgary Winter Olympics a Jamaican team made the country's first ever appearance, hurtling along inside a bobsleigh. It is celebrated in the film *Cool Runnings*.

13

FASTER, HIGHER, FURTHER

PARALYMPICS
THE RACE WITHOUT LIMITS

In 1948 a doctor ran a sports event for people injured during World War 2 (1939-45). In 1960 this became the Paralympics, involving athletes with physical difficulties such as poor mobility, amputations, blindness, and cerebral palsy. The Paralympic Games are run after each summer and winter Olympics. 'Para' means 'next to', which is where the games get their name.

Paralympics today

At the Rio Paralympics in 2016, 4,328 disabled athletes from 160 different countries fought for a total of 528 medals in 22 different event types. These included running, archery, swimming and basketball. As well as being good at their sport, Paralympians need determination, bravery and hard work to achieve their goals.

JONNIE PEACOCK lost his right leg below the knee due to disease when he was five. He became a sprinter and won gold in the 100 metres in the 2012 and 2016 Paralympics.

Hot wheels

There are two main types of wheelchair, which must be operated by using the hand to spin the wheels. Many competitors wear special gloves for better grip and to avoid injuries. The wheels are set at a tilt for extra stability round corners.

- Racing chairs have three wheels and are made from very light materials so they can go as fast as possible. These machines can hurtle along at 30 kilometres per hour in events from sprints to marathons.
- The other kind of wheelchair is used in sports such as rugby and basketball and have at least four wheels – sometimes more so players can tip back without falling over. They are strong but nimble to allow for quick turns and stops during matches.

Artificial limbs

Prosthetics are artificial limbs that allow Paralympians with missing limbs to walk, run, cycle or hold objects. Some are mechanical and use cables and pulleys. Others are myoelectric which means they are worked by signals from the brain. Runners often use blades such as the Flex-Foot, a foot replacement made of carbon fibre that stores and releases energy as the wearer propels forwards.

TANNI GREY-THOMPSON was born with spina bifida and was a wheelchair user from when she was seven. She became a top racer and competed for Britain in five Paralympics, winning 16 medals, including 11 golds, from 100 metre sprints to the 42.19- kilometre marathon.

REINHILD MÖLLER from Germany lost her left leg in an accident when she was three. She became a brilliant fast skier and zoomed to 19 medals in the winter Paralympics. She also ran so well she won four medals sprinting in the summer events!

American swimmer TRISCHA ZORN was born blind and between 1980 and 2004 she set the record for Paralympic medals. She competed in seven Paralympic games and won 55 medals, 41 of them were gold.

FASTER, HIGHER, FURTHER

RIDE! THE RACE TO PEDAL

Bicycles are powered by the rider, but they can get more speed with aerodynamic shape, using light but strong materials… or getting a tow from a car!

Tough race

The toughest bike race is the Tour de France. Competitors cycle more than 128 kilometres along roads, winning prizes for sprints, mountain climbs and being first to the end. The next day they do it again. This goes on for three weeks, finishing in Paris. There are breakaways, bunch finishes, falls, accidents and clashes as nearly 200 riders try to save energy by riding in the slipstream of the bike in front. The overall winner is the rider with the best time for the whole race after about 3,500 kilometres.

The rider leading the Tour de France each day wears a yellow jersey: it's a great honour.

THE TOUR DE FRANCE is a men's only race and there is no women's equivalent. Female cyclists race alongside the men, with no chance of a trophy or financial reward, to raise awareness for this inequality.

Fastest bike

In 2018, Denise Mueller-Korenek attached her bike to a pace-setting dragster car on the Bonneville Salt Flats in Utah, USA, and held on tight. When she was being pulled along at 160 kilometres per hour she released the rope and pedalled as hard as she could. Her bike reached a world-record speed of 296 kilometres per hour, protected from air resistance by the slipstream of the car in front.

No help

The highest speed achieved by a bike without the help of a towing car was 144.18 kilometres per hour by Todd Reichert in 2016. It was an unusual bicycle: he was strapped inside a streamlined carbon fibre shell, lying down to pedal in what is known as a recumbent position. He watched the road ahead via two video cameras.

TODD REICHERT holds the world record for fastest human which he achieved in an Eta speedbike.

DENISE MUELLER-KORENEK holds the world record for paced bicycle land speed.

How to be the fastest

Cyclists are slowed down by air resistance as they push against the atmosphere, while the weight of the bike and their own body also reduces their speed. Racing cyclists try to:

- Wear skin-tight clothing and a streamlined helmet.
- Keep a low body position with elbows tucked in to help slice through the air.
- Ride corners smoothly.
- Brake as little as possible.
- Ride light bikes with cabling stored inside the frame.
- Use wheels with aero-profile spokes and deep-section rims.
- Inflate tyres to a high pressure.

FASTER, HIGHER, FURTHER

DRIVE! THE RACE ON FOUR WHEELS

The first car was the Benz Patent Motor Car that rolled along at 16 kilometres per hour in 1885. It only had three wheels because the single front wheel made it easier to steer. But which is the fastest car today? It depends what you measure: top speed on a straight flat track, in a race, or how quickly the car accelerates.

F1

Formula 1 has the fastest racing cars. They zoom along straight parts of the track, but have to slow down on corners and when they are preparing to overtake rivals. The highest speed ever recorded for an F1 car is currently 372.6 kilometres per hour, a record set by Juan Pablo Montoya in his McLaren-Mercedes in 2005 while practising for the Italian Grand Prix.

Rear wing

Driver

Tyres

How do cars go fast?

F1 cars can whizz along fast because of powerful engines, skilful drivers and, most importantly, their shape. The car's body is very light. It has wings and flaps to create downforce that pushes the tyres onto the track – the opposite of the lifting job that wings do for planes. This downforce is vital on fast corners. Smooth, curved sides also reduce the car's air resistance, known as drag.

Other things that help F1 cars go fast include:

- They have seven types of tyre ranging in hardness and grip that are used for different weather conditions. The tyres are filled with nitrogen instead of air to stay at the right pressure.
- Drivers change gear as quickly as possible by using buttons on the steering wheel rather than the traditional gear stick used on road cars.
- At pit stops, mechanics change tyres and refuel the car in seconds. The record for the fastest pit stop is currently held by Red Bull Racing, who changed all four tyres in just 1.82 seconds during the 2019 Brazilian Grand Prix.

← Pit crew

Front wing

Land speed

Thrust SCC was the first car to break the sound barrier in the Black Rock Desert, Nevada, USA in 1997. The supersonic car was 16.5-metres long and 3.66-metres wide. It reached 1,227.985 kilometres per hour. It was powered by two jet engines – which British driver Andy Green could handle because he was an RAF pilot.

Fastest road car

The Bugatti Veyron Super Sport can go from 0 to 100 kilometres per hour in 2.6 seconds. Its top speed is 431 kilometres per hour and it is the fastest car that can be driven on normal roads. But a special Bugatti Chiron Sport hit 490 kilometres per hour on a German test track.

FASTER, HIGHER, FURTHER

SNOW! THE RACE TO SLIDE

The term 'ski' comes from an ancient word for 'split piece of wood'. This is because the first skis were thin planks strapped under people's feet to allow them to cross frozen marshes and wetlands. The oldest found so far date from about 8000 BC – nearly 5,000 years before we invented the wheel!

Speedy skiers

The fastest skiers compete in speed skiing events where they hurtle in a straight line down a hill. Ivan Origone set the top speed for men at 254.958 kilometres per hour and Sanna Tidstrand set the women's top speed at 242.59 kilometres per hour. That is about as fast as a skydiver freefalling from a plane!

Improvements in skiing equipment help skiers to be faster and better:

SKIS	These were wooden at first, later metal, now they are made of lightweight fibreglass or carbon fibre.
BOOTS	Early leather boots had a raised lip at the toe so the boot could be tied on. From about 1840 a heel strap kept boots in place. Today they are made from plastic.
POLES	Wooden sticks were used with the first skis. Today they are bent to reduce drag and made of carbon.
SNOW GOGGLES	The earliest known goggles date from 2,000 years ago and were made from bone with a narrow slit to see through and avoid the Sun's glare.
CHAIRLIFT	The chairlift was invented in 1936 and led to skiing becoming a leisure activity.

Sliding sports

If you've clung to a sled zooming down a snowy hill, you'll know it can be exciting and a bit scary. How would you cope with these events?

BOBSLEIGH Teams ride a streamlined sled down a narrow, twisting icy track. Speeds vary on different courses and depending on how many riders are in the sled, but they often reach around 150 kilometres per hour.

LUGE Competitors lie face first on a thin sled and hurtle down the ice track. The fastest recorded speed was 150.42 kilometres per hour by Frank Williams (USA) in Canada in 2017.

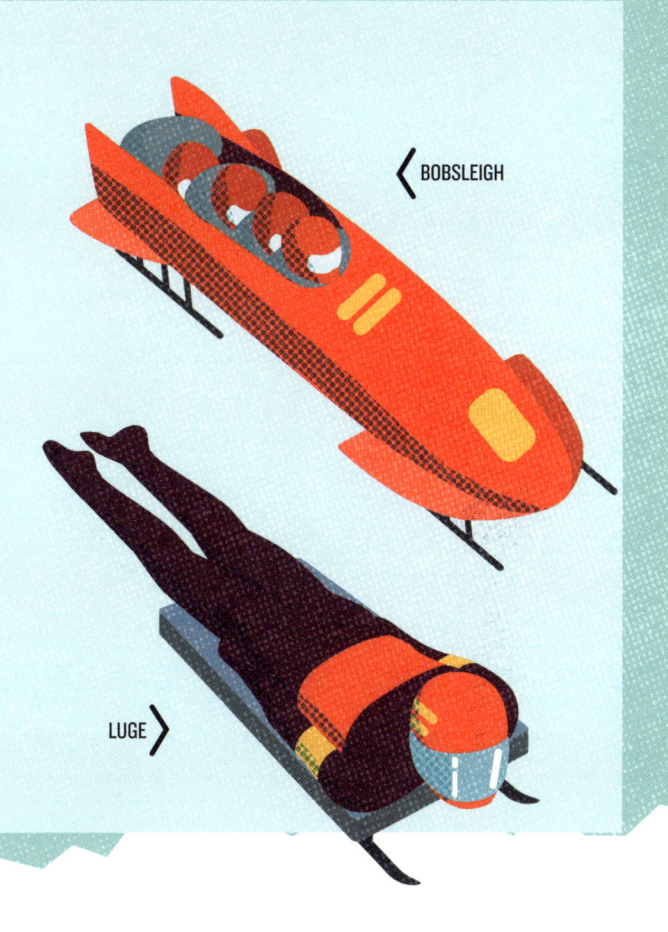

< BOBSLEIGH

LUGE >

Ice Race

The world's most famous dog sled race is the Iditarod, run across Alaska over different courses of about 1,700 kilometres. It always ends in Nome because it is run to remember a heroic journey by dog-pulled sleds to deliver medicines to the town in 1925.

Skates

The first ice skates were made by strapping animal leg bones under the feet about 5,000 years ago. Wood and metal were then used but 1914 saw the arrival of the first blade made from one piece of metal. This made skates lighter, but stronger.

- The top speed in a skating race is 54.4 kilometres per hour by Kjeld Nuis in the 2019 Speed Skating World Cup Final.

- Figure skaters dance and spin and the invention of the toe pick around 1870 allowed them to stop and turn quickly because it had lots of tiny teeth to grip the ice. The fastest spin was by Olivia Oliver in 2015 when she performed at a dizzying 342 turns per minute.

22

JOURNEYS AND EXPEDITIONS

Humans love making discoveries. All throughout history, people have left their homes to explore new places. We trekked across continents and conquered Earth's highest mountains, from boiling deserts to freezing Poles. Then we soared into the sky to see worlds beyond our own.

JOURNEYS AND EXPEDITIONS

TRADE! THE RACE TO LINK EAST AND WEST

People raced to connect the world even before we knew how big it was. Europe in the west and Asia in the east traded goods and swapped ideas for more than 2,000 years, even though they are separated by mountains and vast lands.

Silk and spice

A set of trading routes between China and Europe crossed the mountains and deserts of Central Asia. Few people travelled the whole way, as it was a tough and sometimes dangerous journey. Instead they carted their valuable goods part of the way and sold them to merchants. This was called the 'Silk Road' after the soft fabric that originally came from China. The later sea routes between East and West were called 'Spice Routes'. Spices, such as pepper, did not grow in Europe. They were valuable as they helped to make food tastier, were burned as incense to make the air smell nice, and were used in some medicines.

Marco Polo

In 1271, Italian merchants Niccolò and Maffeo Polo trekked along the Silk Road to China along with Niccolò's 17-year-old son, Marco. For four years they struggled across deserts, suffering illnesses and many hardships. When they reached China, Marco learned four languages, and was taken on as an important official by Kublai Khan, a powerful leader. He travelled across the huge Mongol empire and covered 39,000 kilometres by the time he finally returned to Italy in 1295. His writings became the Western world's best record of Eastern achievements when China later stopped contact with the rest of the world.

Trade boom

People raced east for more than silk and spices. Among the items first traded from the East were paper, around 1150, which led to writing becoming key for communication. Gunpowder was another Chinese invention to reach Europe by the end of the 13th century. It later meant wars were fought with cannons and guns rather than bows and arrows. But perhaps as important was the exchange of ideas about science, religion and art.

New ideas

Western explorers admired many other things first developed in China, and they were slowly brought back to Europe.

COAL People burned this special rock for heat. It was not widely used in the west until the 18th century.

MAGNETIC COMPASS A device used to navigate, with a needle that always showed north. It was used in China from the end of the 12th century.

ASBESTOS An amazing material that did not burn. It wasn't mined in the West until the 19th century, when it was used for insulation. However, we now know that asbestos is harmful to humans.

A POSTAL SYSTEM One that used teams of horse riders. This idea was used by the Romans as well as the Chinese, but it didn't catch on in Europe until 1660.

PORCELAIN A type of strong, white pottery that was often beautifully decorated. It took until 1575 for Europeans to learn to make it themselves.

PAPER MONEY The first European bank notes didn't appear until the 1660s.

JOURNEYS AND EXPEDITIONS

CHRISTOPHER COLUMBUS
THE RACE ACROSS THE ATLANTIC

Why do so many South American countries speak Spanish? How did the 'West Indies' islands and the original 'American Indians' get these names when they are nowhere near India? The answer takes us to Christopher Columbus who caused all this without even knowing it!

Christopher Columbus was an Italian sailor who set out to find a route to Asia from Europe. The Silk Road that carried spices and silk from Asia to Europe became difficult to cross in the 15th century because new rulers took over some of its key points. So European traders looked for other routes to reach Asia. Sailing south took them towards dangerously stormy seas around Africa. But Christopher Columbus had an idea: since the Earth was round, he could sail west across the Atlantic Ocean until he hit Asia. He believed that if he stayed south the winds would take him west towards his target. To get home, he would head north where winds blowing the other way would fill his sails for the return trip.

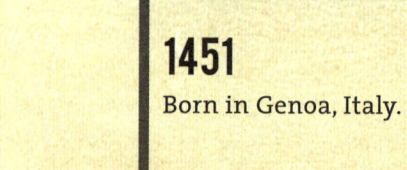

It was a good plan. But Columbus didn't realise that the distances were far greater than he had calculated, or that there was another huge continent in the way! Columbus sailed west and finally reached land. The sailors believed that they were in Asia, but they had actually landed on an island in the Bahamas. Because Columbus thought he had reached Asia, he called the people he met there 'Indians'! Actually they were in the Americas, home to about 100 million people at the time.

TIMELINE OF COLUMBUS'S LIFE:

1451
Born in Genoa, Italy.

1476
Moved to Portugal and from there sailed to many lands.

1485
He moved to Spain to get money for his expeditions.

Columbus was hailed as a hero for finding a sailing route to Asia. He made three more trips along a similar route, finding more new lands, and became the first European to set foot in South America. His feat of navigation and determination changed the world. Over the following decades, the leading sea powers of Spain and Portugal realised what he had not: that this was not Asia, but was a whole 'New World'. They invaded, building empires and removing huge amounts of gold and silver. Sadly, many of the people they encountered died either in battle or from illnesses carried by the European invaders. The conquerors also started to explore a massive land mass to the north, which is now the USA.

1492
On 3rd August he set off with three ships and 90 men, heading west in an attempt to reach Asia. They reached islands near (modern-day) North America 70 days later.

1493
On January 16th Columbus set off back to Spain with his news, as well as the pineapples and turkeys he had found.

1493–1504
Columbus returned to America three times.

1506
Columbus died, still thinking he had found a route to Asia.

JOURNEYS AND EXPEDITIONS

SAIL! THE RACE AROUND THE WORLD

Travelling around the world 500 years ago was a great achievement, because there were no maps to show the way. It was, literally, a journey into the unknown.

Spice race

The land routes between Europe and Asia shut in 1453. Now Europeans would have to cross the seas to trade for spices. In 1488, Bartholomew Diaz headed east by sea, but storms blew his ship round the southern tip of Africa, and his terrified crew refused to sail on. The first person to successfully sail directly from Europe to India was Vasco da Gama in 1497. He sailed east on a route around Africa.

Magellan

The first sucessful trip all the way around the world was led by Ferdinand Magellan, a Portuguese sailor who was paid by rival nation Spain to try the trip. Unlike Diaz and da Gama, Magellan went west, following the lead of Columbus. He believed that sailing west would take him to Asia. His fleet of five ships and 260 crew left on 20th September, 1519. There were many challenges throughout the journey:

SHIPWRECKS
They were in uncharted waters and did not know about hidden rocks, which caused many shipwrecks.

ARGUMENTS
Magellan had one captain executed, and one ship abandoned the trip and went home, carrying vital supplies.

MALNUTRITION
The crew had only dry 'biscuit' food and salted meat to eat on the long journey. The lack of fruit and vegetables made their gums swell up until their teeth fell out – an illness called scurvy.

WAR
Magellan did not pass any islands crossing the Pacific, but when they did eventually find land, he got involved in a local war, which led to him being speared to death.

Return

Only one ship from Magellan's fleet, with 18 exhausted and relieved crew, made it back to Spain on 6th September 1522, led by replacement captain Juan Sebastián Elcano. The voyage had shown the size of our world and that it could be crossed on the seas. It also opened up a new route to Asia, and triggered trade with islands in the Pacific.

JOURNEYS AND EXPEDITIONS

ELLEN MACARTHUR THE SOLO RACE

How would you like to steer a small boat across a huge ocean with roaring winds tearing at the sails and giant waves smashing into the sides so hard you must hold on just to stand up? These are some of the challenges of sailing round the world on your own. The first woman to do it was Ellen MacArthur.

Ellen was born in England in 1976 a long way from the sea. When she was a child, her aunt took her sailing and she fell in love with it. She read library books on how to sail and saved her money to buy her own dinghy. When she was 19, she sailed alone around Britain in a 6.4-metre dinghy. In 2001 she finished second in the incredibly hard Vendée Globe race and became the youngest woman to sail around the world.

Then she set herself a new challenge: the fastest journey around the Earth's oceans powered only by the wind. To do this she needed to be able to do far more than sail the boat: *"You have to be able to repair the engine, or to sew your arm up if you cut it open!"* She set a new world record when she reached land again after 71 days, 14 hours and 18 minutes on 7th February 2005.

The Vendée Globe

The Vendée Globe Trophy is the hardest prize in sailing: a single-handed non-stop journey around the world without any help. It began in 1989 and is named after the Vendée part of France where it starts and ends every four years. Competitors follow what is called the 'Clipper Route' between Europe and Oceania, passing Africa's Cape of Good Hope and the famously stormy Cape Horn. Clippers were ships racing to bring tea back from China that were powered by sails hanging from three masts to harness as much wind as possible.

JOURNEYS AND EXPEDITIONS

1521
Ferdinand Magellan (see page 28) tried to measure the depth of the Pacific Ocean but his 61-metre weighted line did not touch the bottom.

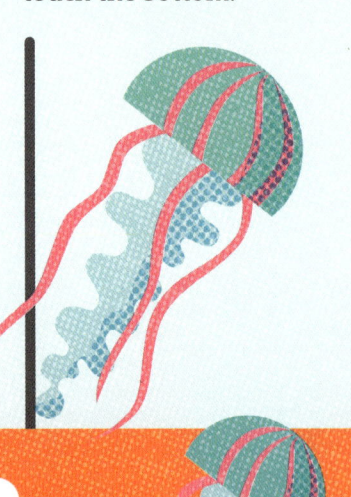

1818
Sir John Ross found the first evidence of deep-sea life by catching worms and jellyfish about 2,000 metres down.

1872–1876
Charles Wyville Thomson conducted the first deep sea exploration expedition on HMS Challenger.

1930
William Beebe and Otis Barton boarded the steel Bathysphere to become the first humans to visit the deep sea.

1960
Jacques Piccard and Don Walsh, with the submersible Trieste, descended to the bottom of the Challenger Deep in the Mariana Trench (10.7 kilometres deep), and saw fish living there.

THE UNDERWORLD
The race to the bottom of the sea

1776
American David Bushnell built an early form of submersible craft and tried to attack a British ship during the War of Independence.

1857
James Alden discovered the first known submarine valley, California's Monterey Canyon.

1943
Jacques Cousteau and Emile Gagnan created the aqualung, allowing divers to breath underwater.

1954
The first manned, untethered, research submersible FNRS-3 descended to 4,041 metres.

1995
Geosat satellite radar data was made public and allowed global mapping of the sea floor.

2017
An international team announced it will try to map the entire ocean floor by 2030.

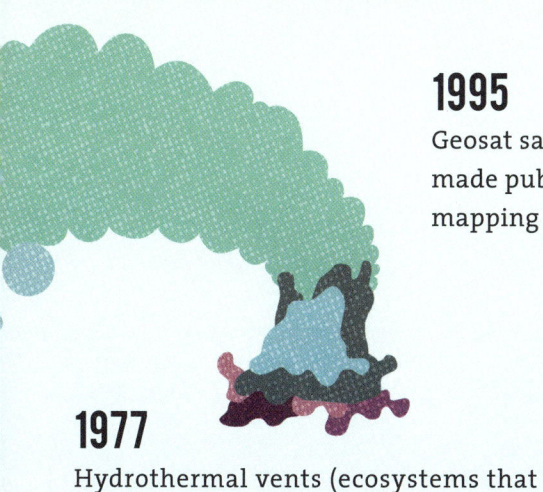

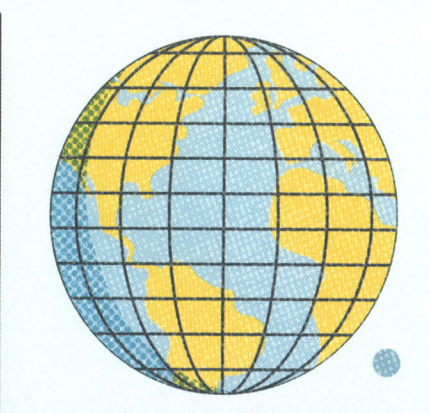

1977
Hydrothermal vents (ecosystems that use chemical rather than solar energy) were discovered by a team led by Robert Ballard.

1997
The deepest ever free dive with no equipment was made by Herbert Nichst who used weights to descend to 214 metres.

We know less about the ocean seabed than we do about our galaxy. Deep undersea exploration is really hard: there is hardly any light below 200 metres, and deep-water pressure would crush our unprotected bodies. We have visited the deepest ocean floor, but only 7 per cent of the ocean below 200 metres has been mapped.

1985
Ballard's team found the famous shipwrecked *Titanic* more than 3,810 metres down in the Atlantic.

2012
James Cameron completed the first solo dive to the bottom of the Challenger Deep in the Mariana Trench.

1979
American Sylvia Earle set the world untethered diving record as she dropped 381 metres in a special diving suit.

2005
Chikyu, a deep-sea drilling vessel, was completed. It has since investigated below the seabed and there are plans to drill through 7.5 kilometres of the Earth's crust beneath 2.5 kilometres of water and to reach the interior of our planet, called the mantle.

33

JOURNEYS AND EXPEDITIONS

DAVID LIVINGSTONE
THE RACE ACROSS AFRICA

In the 19th century Europeans began exploring beyond the coasts of Africa. They wanted to see its plants and animals, to trade, and to find the sources of great rivers such as the Nile. Some also aimed to spread the Christian faith and to take over lands as European nations built empires around the world.

David Livingstone came from a poor family in Glasgow, Scotland. He worked 14 hours every day, except Sunday, in a cotton mill from the age of 10, and at night he studied, educating himself. He became a doctor and wanted to explore new lands and spread the Christian faith.

In his work and expeditions from 1841 to 1873 Livingstone was interested in Africa's way of life and languages, as well as working to free people from slavery. He usually travelled with just a few helpers to make sure that he was not seen as a threat by those he met, so local tribes often helped him. Many other explorers went in large groups and were more interested in riches and glory.

One of Livingstone's trips was incredibly tough. Sick and short of food, he could have taken a ship home, but he refused because the porters who helped him would have to become slaves once he left. He wrote that the best way to end slavery was "civilisation, commerce and Christianity". He believed that faith in God, trade and making life fairer for all would make the world a better place.

The first humans

The human race began in Africa. The earliest fossils of *Homo sapiens* – humans – date back to 315,000 years ago and were found in Ethiopia in Africa. About 120,000 years ago their descendants (us!) started to leave the continent and settle around the world.

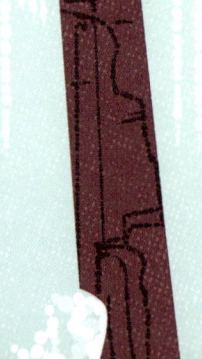

Livingstone's achievements

- He was the first European to cross southern Africa from coast to coast.
- He was the first European to see the Zambezi River where he named the spectacular Victoria Falls after Britain's queen in 1855.
- He campaigned against the cruel African slave trade.
- His books described Africa to Europeans.

When Livingstone died, his heart was buried by a tree in what is now Zambia. His tomb is in Westminster Abbey in London.

JOURNEYS AND EXPEDITIONS

HEAT! THE RACE ACROSS AUSTRALIA

Aboriginal peoples have lived in Australia for 40,000 years. They coped with its challenging landscape of mountains, marshes, deserts and furnace-like heat. When Europeans arrived they found the conditions really tough as they tried to conquer a continent.

Past the Blue Mountains

The first European to land in Australia was Dutchman Willem Janszoon in 1606. But European settlers did not arrive until 1788. They were from England and only occupied a narrow strip of coastal land, blocked by the massive Blue Mountains, part of the Great Dividing Range. Explorers got past the Blue Mountains in 1813, and then the race was on to cross the full continent.

Burke's expedition

In 1860 the South Australian government offered a £2,000 reward for getting across the middle of Australia – partly to set up a telegraph line. Robert Burke took up the challenge. He set off from Melbourne with 19 men, 20 tons of supplies, horses, and camels specially transported from India to help cross the desert. Here's what happened on their journey:

20 AUGUST 1860
Burke's expedition began.

16 DECEMBER 1860
The expedition reached Cooper Creek. Burke, Wills, King and Gray set off further north, leaving William Brahe in charge at Cooper Creek.

11 FEBRUARY 1861
Burke's group were blocked by swamp flats on the Flinders River, so couldn't reach the sea.

17 APRIL 1861
Gray died in Stony Desert on the group's return journey to Cooper Creek.

21 APRIL 1861
Delayed by burying Gray's body, the three men reached the camp just after Brahe had gone. They found buried supplies and left a note in the same spot before continuing their journey.

Prize winner

The prize for the first crossing went to John Stuart. He led six expeditions into Australia, often looking for lands to graze sheep. Stuart became expert at life in the 'bush', and often went ahead of his group to check the route, using only a compass and a watch for navigation – there were no maps. On the return journey of his prize winning route, his eyesight failed and he lay on a stretcher carried between two horses for about 950 kilometres.

SWAMPS that blocked Burke's path to the sea.

STONY DESERT

COOPER CREEK

MELBOURNE

8 MAY 1861
Brahe returned to check Cooper Creek but did not find the note.

LATE JUNE 1861
Burke and Wills died. King met a local tribe and lived with them for several months.

SEPTEMBER 1861
King was rescued.

Aborigines

Central Australia is mostly hot, dry desert where food and water are scarce. Australia's first people – known as Aborigines – lived in it for tens of thousands of years before Europeans came.

JOURNEYS AND EXPEDITIONS

AMUNDSEN VS. SCOTT
THE RACE TO THE SOUTH POLE

Whose was the greater achievement? Roald Amundsen reaching the South Pole first, or Robert Scott's arrival a few weeks later? You decide.

In the early 20th century, Arctic explorers raced to be first to stand at the North Pole (Arctic) or South Pole (Antarctica). They had to trek across icy wildernesses that offered no food or shelter. It was incredibly tough. Two explorers, Roald Amundsen from Norway and Robert Scott from the UK, led expeditions to be the first humans to reach the South Pole, in 1910. Here's what happened on the two journeys:

Amundsen

7 JUNE 1910
Amundsen's ship *Fram* set sail from Norway. He led a team of 19, including skiers and dog-sledders. His aim was speed.

14 JANUARY 1911
Arrived at the Bay of Whales 96.5 kilometres nearer the Pole than Scott.

18 OCTOBER 1911
Amundsen and four others set out. They had good weather and travelled quickly on skis and four sleds pulled by husky dogs. They kept going as fast as they could at an average of 24 kilometres a day.

Scott

15 JUNE 1910
His ship *Terra Nova* sailed from Cardiff, Wales. He took a team of 65, including many scientists.

4 JANUARY 1911
Arrived at Ross Island. They took their time preparing as they did not know they were in a race.

1 NOVEMBER 1911
Scott and four others left their base camp. They wore padded boots or snowshoes and pulled their sleds themselves. They stopped to measure weather conditions and collect rock specimens. The average per day was 21 kilometres.

AMUNDSEN was a Norwegian explorer who had planned to be first to the North Pole and learned how to survive in extreme cold from Arctic Inuit people. But after American Robert Peary reached that target first in 1909, Amundsen secretly changed his plan. Only his brother knew he intended to try for the South Pole instead.

SCOTT was a British Royal Navy Captain who first travelled to the Antarctic in 1902. He planned his expedition as a copy of Shackleton's attempt in 1908, which used only manpower and ponies with no skis or dogs and had stopped only 156 kilometres short.

14 DECEMBER 1911
They reached the South Pole, put up the Norwegian flag and left a tent with messages for Scott. By the time Scott reached the pole, Amundsen was already back at base camp. They sent a message to Scott saying "Congratulations" from the kings of Norway and Britain. Amundsen went on more Arctic expeditions until he disappeared in 1928 on a mission to rescue other explorers.

17 JANUARY 1912
Scott was shocked when he found the flag and tent at the South Pole. On the return journey, the team was hit by extreme weather such as blizzards.

29 MARCH 1912
Scott's last diary entry. He and his men had died one by one, tired, hungry and suffering terribly. They were only 18 kilometres from the supply base. His diary was found in their tent the next year and many admired the bravery it showed.

The last entry in Scott's diary read:

'It seems a pity, but I do not think I can write more.'

39

JOURNEYS AND EXPEDITIONS

AMELIA EARHART
THE RACE ACROSS THE SKY

Amelia Earhart led two races: one was to fly across the world and the other was for women to be seen as just as capable as men. Her bravery and skill made her America's most famous female pilot.

Amelia was born in 1897, six years before the first powered flight by an aircraft even happened. She got in a plane when she was 23, loved it and wrote: "*I knew I had to fly*". She was among the first women to qualify as a pilot in the US.

She is best known for flying solo from Canada to Ireland in 1932. It took nearly 15 hours as she coped with bad weather, thick cloud making it hard to see, and ice coating the windshield and wings. She was only the second person to fly alone across the Atlantic after Charles Lindbergh in 1927.

Amelia Earhart disappeared in 1937 during her attempt to be the first pilot to fly all the way around the world. Her plane was never found.

Amelia's first plane was yellow so she called it 'The Canary' like the bird.

40

Earhart the record-breaker

- First woman to fly across the Atlantic (she was navigator) in 1928
- First pilot to fly over the Pacific from Hawaii to California
- First pilot to cross America coast to coast

JOURNEYS AND EXPEDITIONS

NORGAY & HILLARY
THE RACE TO THE TOP

In 1953, Tenzing Norgay and Edmund Hillary achieved the greatest challenge in mountain climbing: reaching the top of 8,850-metre-tall Mount Everest.

By 1953, at least nine expeditions had tried and failed to reach the top of Everest. No wonder: the area above 8,000 metres is called a 'Death Zone' because no animals or plants can live on it. Climbers carry everything they need to climb the icy rock where one slip could kill, including an oxygen tank to help them breathe in the high, thin air. They sleep on narrow, snow-covered ledges between climbs.

EDMUND HILLARY was from New Zealand and always loved climbing.

TENZING NORGAY was a Sherpa, born close to Everest. He had been a guide on six expeditions already.

42

Tenzing and Hillary were part of the ninth British expedition to Everest. The team was well planned and equipped: ten climbers were helped by 350 porters who carried 13 tons of supplies, plus 20 local guides. The team set off on 10th March, stopping off at a series of camps to rest, to get used to breathing the thin air, and to store supplies.

On 26th May two climbers from the team headed for the top. But Tom Bourdillon and Charles Evans turned back when they were only 101 metres from the summit because they were exhausted and running out of oxygen. Now Hillary and Tenzing would try.

The duo spent the night of 28th May in a wind-blown tent, suffering temperatures of -27°C. They began the final climb at 4am. They barely spoke because every word was an effort in the freezing, thin air. But seven gruelling hours later they shook hands and hugged on the top of the world. They had made it.

Top challenges

Other mountains are harder to climb than Everest because they have steep cliffs and other difficulties. But Everest is the world's highest mountain. About 5,000 climbers have stood on its summit, whilst hundreds have died trying. The first woman to conquer Everest was Japanese climber Junko Tabei in 1975.

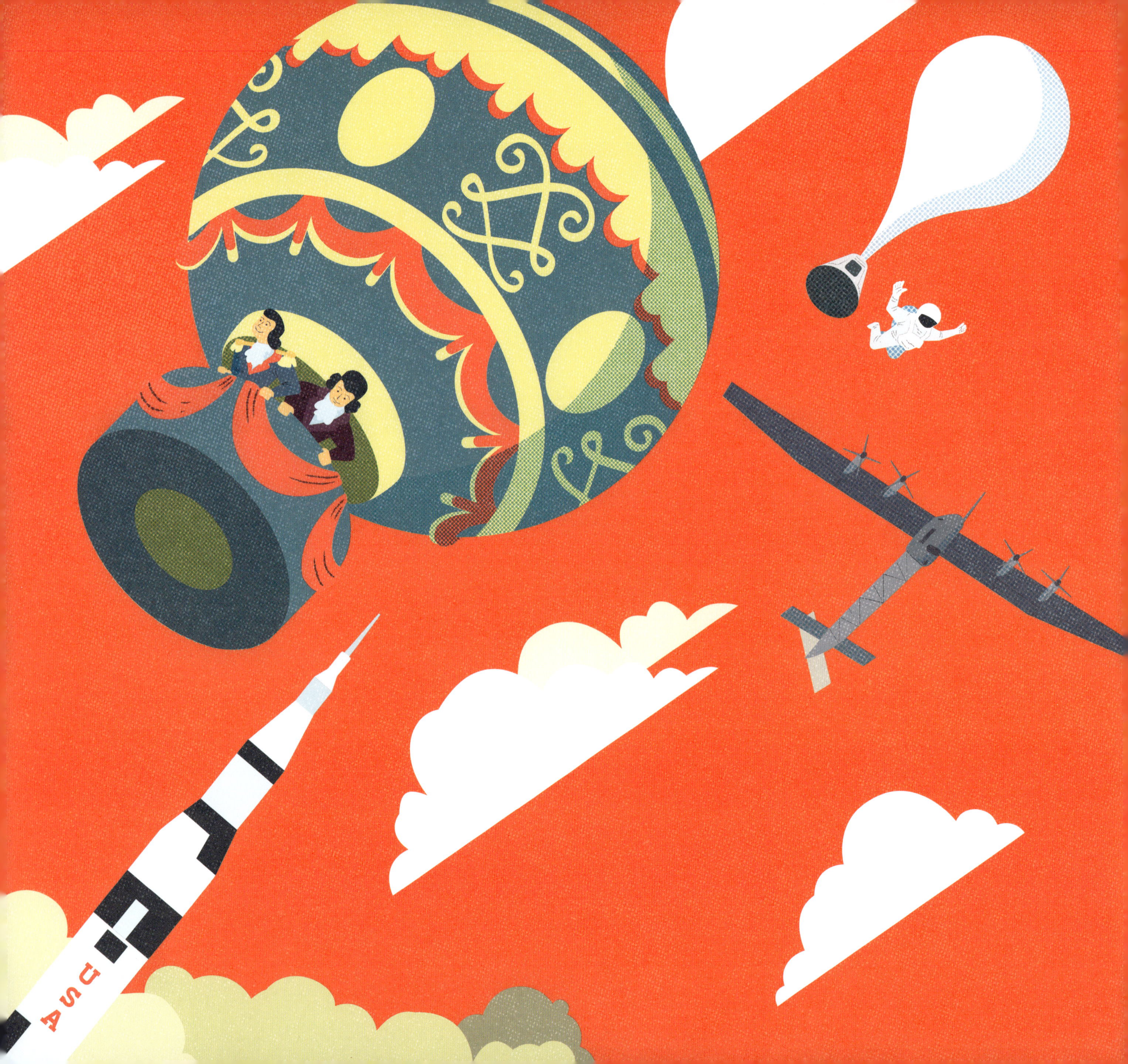
USA

TRANSPORT AND VEHICLES

Human transport started with the invention of the wheel. This allowed us to roll further and faster. Soon we learned to travel across land, sea and through the skies. For power, we used our bodies and the wind, then fuels like coal and oil. Today's challenge is to use sustainable sources of fuel such as the Sun's rays.

TRANSPORT AND VEHICLES

SHIPS THE RACE TO SAIL

Humans first learnt to sail on rivers and along coasts. Our planet is mostly covered by water, and we have been crossing the oceans for thousands of years – most human exploration and migration was by sea until about 100 years ago.

RAFT
The first boats were probably rafts made with wood or animal skin. Later we developed kayaks and dugouts. Early migrations included long crossings between the Pacific islands.

OAR
The earliest known oars are about 7,000 years old, but they probably existed much earlier.

KEEL
This long beam along the bottom of a boat supports it in rough weather. It allowed the Vikings to travel across the North Sea from Scandinavia to Britain. They first arrived in 793 AD.

SAIL
Sailboats that use the wind for power date as far back as 4000 BC, when boats floated downstream and used the wind to sail against the current on the River Nile in north Africa.

LATEEN SAIL
This is a triangular sail set at an angle which allows boats to zig-zag in any direction, rather than only with the wind. The sail dates from at least 100 BC.

CARAVEL
This had two or three masts with lateen sails and was the type of small but strong ship used to explore the oceans (see pages 26-29 – Columbus and Magellan) from the late 15th century. It could sail in shallow waters, such as along rivers, and was great for exploring.

46

STEAM POWER
From 1819, steam engines helped power ships across the Atlantic, although they had to carry mountains of heavy coal to power them. Funnels started to replace masts and sails.

HOVERCRAFT
These ride on a cushion of air, so they can move easily from land to water. The first proper hovercraft floated on top of the waves in 1959.

Where am I?
It's hard to know where you are on the open seas. Early sailors stayed in sight of the coast, but soon learnt to use the Sun and the stars to judge their position. From about 550AD carved brass instruments called astrolabes helped sailors find their latitude, allowing navigators to estimate the time and their position on the sea. Compasses to show the direction of North were invented in China in the 12th century, and their use spread west.

IRON/PROPELLER
In 1845 the *Great Britain* was the first iron-hulled ship to cross the Atlantic powered by another innovation, the screw propeller.

SOLAR POWER
In 2012, the *Tûranor PlanetSolar* was the first vehicle powered by photovoltaic solar cells to travel around the world.

47

TRANSPORT AND VEHICLES

CARS THE RACE ON FOUR WHEELS

Cars made it far easier for people to travel where and when they wanted. They developed from steam-driven wagons to vehicles powered by petrol, diesel or electricity.

Gradual development

The first car was made by German engineer Karl Benz in 1885. It had three wheels and the engine was under the driver's seat. The wheels were turned by a chain, like a bicycle! Soon, four-wheeled cars with engines at the front were built. Other improvements around this time included adding a steering wheel to replace a ship-style tiller, and adding an enclosed cabin to keep out rain and wind. For a long time, cars had to be hand-started by turning a handle until the invention of the starter motor allowed drivers to turn a switch instead.

BENZ first motorwagen.

Engine moves to the front of the car.

48

Mass production

From 1910, Henry Ford made millions of cars very cheaply for the first time. How did he do it?

- He had factories where each person did the same job on every car as they moved slowly along an assembly line.
- From 1915-25 he only used black paint because it dried faster than other colours.
- His assembly lines meant that, instead of taking 12 hours, it took 93 minutes to make a car.
- His most famous car was the Model T. In 19 years he sold 15,500,000 in the United States, nearly a million in Canada, and 250,000 in Great Britain. This was half of all the new cars in world.

Engine change

A carburettor turns liquid petrol into mist that is mixed with air and ignited in petrol-driven engines. This was a major advance on earlier steam, gas and electric-powered engines because it was lighter, safer and more powerful. Early engines had pistons that went up and down inside cylinders. From 1964 this changed to the rotary engine, which has moving parts that spin.

Different fuels

Fossil fuels such as petrol and diesel are bad for the environment and the climate. Alternatives already on the roads include electric cars, often powered by a fuel cell that uses hydrogen or oxygen to convert chemical energy to electrical energy.

Changing roads

Motorists bought petrol in cans from shops until the first filling station opened in America in 1893. More cars meant busier roads, so roundabouts were introduced from 1909 and traffic lights for cars first appeared in 1914, in America. The first motorways were built in Germany in the 1920s, to allow people to travel long distances much faster. Years later, in 1949, zebra crossings were added, for pedestrians to improve safety. All of these things combine to make the modern road systems we know today.

Modern cars have comfortable cabins.

TRANSPORT AND VEHICLES

BIKES THE RACE ON TWO WHEELS

The bicycle has been roughly the same shape for 150 years, developing from James Starley's Safety Bicycle in 1885. The Safety Bicycle got its name because it was far easier to ride than previous bikes. Starley invented the frame shape and added other technology to make his bicycle more useable than those before it.

Before Starley

The bicycle developed from the draisine, a wooden frame on which a rider sat between two in-line wheels. They would push off with their feet and could then glide until more steps were needed. When pedals were finally added, the rider had to sit on top of the front wheel to pedal it, such as on a penny farthing.

DRAISINE

PENNY FARTHING

BRAKES
The first brakes (from 1876) were calipers (hinged legs) that slowed the wheel's edges using friction. The latest type of brakes are discs, which work on the middle of the wheel.

TYRES
The first bicycles were called 'boneshakers' because the ride was so bumpy. Then wooden wheels became metal, and solid rubber was added to the outside. Tyres became air-filled from 1889 and rides were smoother!

CHAIN
From 1879 the pedals were attached to a chain that linked to the rear wheel. Machines with cogs and chains were first suggested in the 15th century, while later steam engines sometimes used belts to transfer power – a similar idea.

GEARS
Adding toothed wheels of different sizes made it easier to cycle up hills and to go faster on level ground. The first chain-driven bicycle appeared in 1879.

PEDALS
Modern pedals allowed the rider to sit between the wheels, rather than on top of the front one. The first modern-style pedals in 1840 were attached to treadles, which were levers that sent power to the rear wheel.

Stronger, lighter, faster

While the shape has stayed almost the same, modern bikes have changed. They are now made with stronger, lighter materials and every part has been improved to help riders travel faster and more safely.

51

TRANSPORT AND VEHICLES

600 BC
The Ancient Greeks pulled wooden wagons along tracks carved into stone. Later in Europe, donkeys, horses or children hauled carts along similar tracks or wooden rails.

1774
James Watt improved the design of the steam engine.

1830
The first passenger railway opened between Liverpool and Manchester in September 1830. The railway used Stephenson's *Rocket* locomotive, which had a top speed of 58 kilometres per hour. Railways spread across Britain, replacing the network of canals that had been the best way to carry large loads for a century.

TRAINS
The rolling story

1712
Thomas Newcomen built the first successful steam engine. This stationary machine was used for pumping water from coal mines.

1803
Richard Trevithick put a steam engine on wheels and built the first locomotive, used for carrying coal or rock at mines and ironworks.

1840
Clocks in Britain were set to the same time so that train timetables could be used. The same happened in North America and India as their rail networks developed. Cities grew because people could live further from where they worked. Telegraph poles went up alongside railway lines to improve communication and avoid crashes.

1994

The channel tunnel was opened, linking Great Britain to the European mainland. Travellers now had an alternative method of transport other than boarding a ferry to cross the English Channel.

1863

The world's first underground passenger trains rolled under London. They were very smoky until they switched to electric power from 1890. Subway systems are found today in cities all around the world.

Before trains, transport was very slow. Locomotives made it easy for people to travel long distances, encouraged new technology to be developed and completely changed daily life.

1869

A 3,077 kilometre-long train line was completed across the United States. Engineers learned to blast tunnels and build long, strong bridges to carry heavy trains. Diesel and electricity replaced steam power.

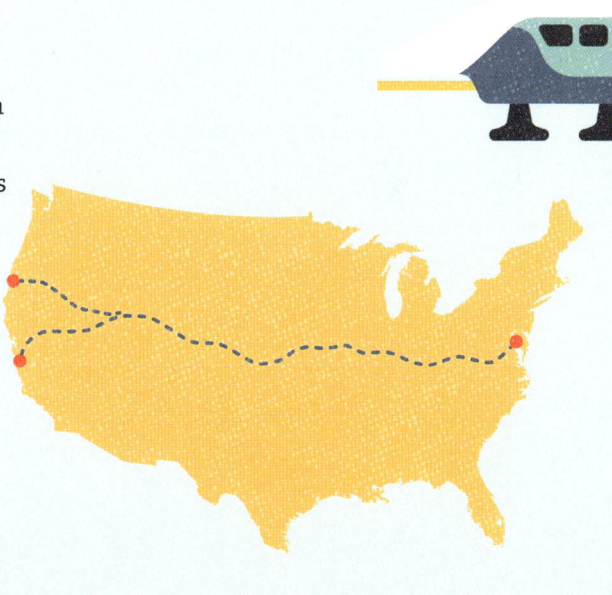

2003

China's Shanghai Maglev, the world's fastest passenger train, ran for the first time. The train has a top speed of 431 kilometres per hour. 'Floating' maglev (short for 'magnetically levitated') trains don't have wheels. They use magnetic power to lift and power them along the tracks, which uses less fuel than diesel or electric trains.

TRANSPORT AND VEHICLES

BALLOONS THE RACE INTO THE SKY

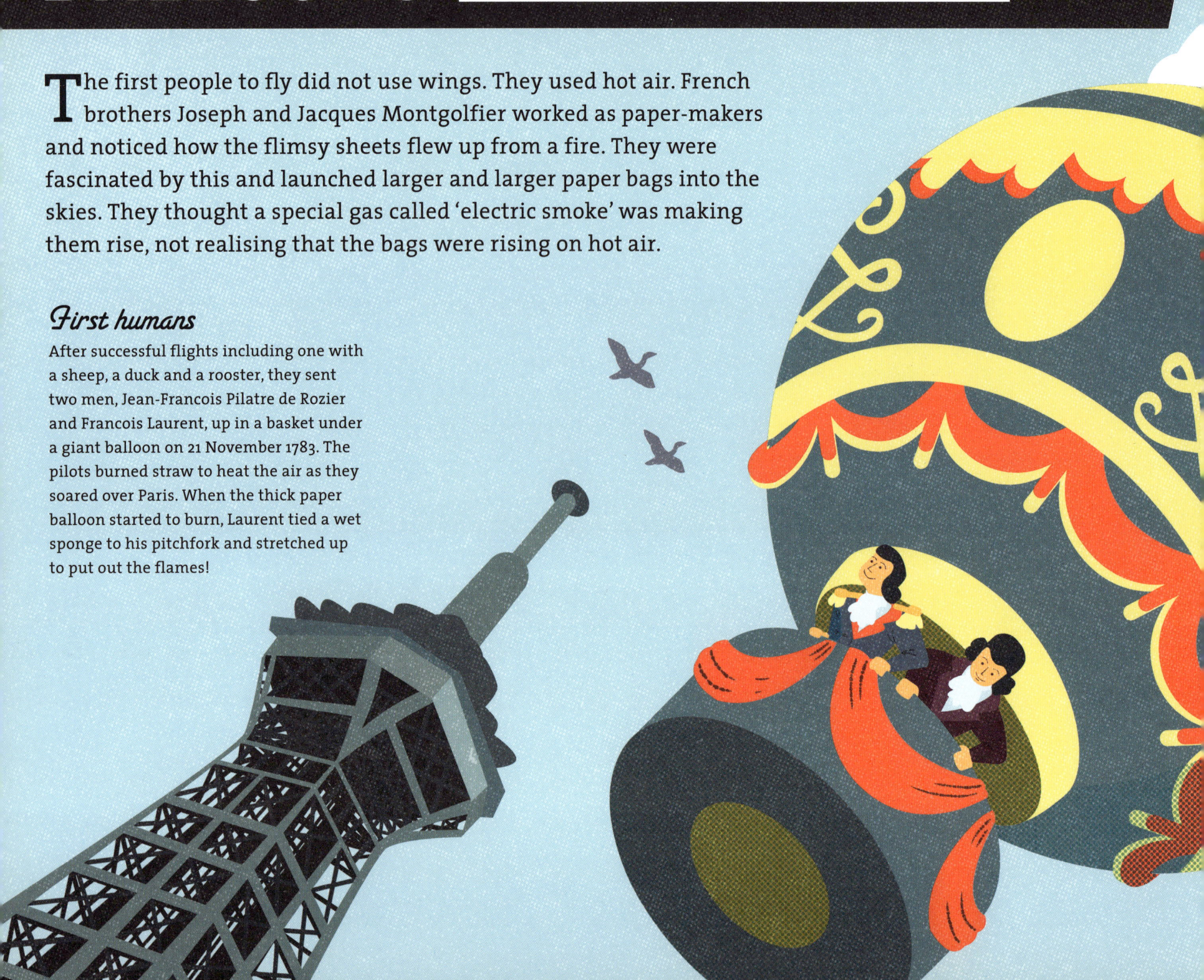

The first people to fly did not use wings. They used hot air. French brothers Joseph and Jacques Montgolfier worked as paper-makers and noticed how the flimsy sheets flew up from a fire. They were fascinated by this and launched larger and larger paper bags into the skies. They thought a special gas called 'electric smoke' was making them rise, not realising that the bags were rising on hot air.

First humans

After successful flights including one with a sheep, a duck and a rooster, they sent two men, Jean-Francois Pilatre de Rozier and Francois Laurent, up in a basket under a giant balloon on 21 November 1783. The pilots burned straw to heat the air as they soared over Paris. When the thick paper balloon started to burn, Laurent tied a wet sponge to his pitchfork and stretched up to put out the flames!

A huge craze for ballooning began. Some pilots did not use hot air but the newly discovered gas hydrogen, which rises because it is very light.

The highest ever skydive started from a balloon in 2012 when Felix Baumgartner leaped out at 39,000 metres high. He fell faster than the speed of sound for 10 minutes, reaching 1,342 kilometres per hour before opening his parachute to land in the desert of New Mexico.

In 1797 a balloon burst while flying over Paris. The pilot escaped with the help of a new invention: the parachute.

In 1999 Bertrand Piccard and Brian Jones flew a balloon around the world. They covered 40,814 kilometres in 19 days, 21 hours, and 55 minutes to complete the longest flight. They were kept afloat by hot air and another lightweight gas, helium.

55

TRANSPORT AND VEHICLES

WRIGHT BROTHERS THE RACE TO FLY

When brothers Orville and Wilbur Wright were growing up, they loved playing with a toy helicopter powered by rubber bands. Later, inspired by pictures of gliders and studying birds, they used their practical skills as bicycle makers to build the first flying machine.

Orville was born in 1867 and his brother arrived four years later. Their family moved around lots and they did not do well at school, but were very close to each other. As adults, they set up a bicycle repair shop and realised they could build better machines than the ones they repaired.

They experimented with kites and gliders, launching them over sand dunes for soft landings. The brothers learned fast and added modifications to existing designs, including:

- a rudder at the back to help steer the plane like a ship
- a horizontal flap to add lift
- shaped wings so that air flowed round the glider, helping to keep it up

The brothers tested these ideas in a wind tunnel – another new invention. Now they needed power. They had an engine specially built to be as light as possible. It turned two propellers that blasted air backwards to push their craft along.

On 17th December 1903 they made the first human-powered flight in a machine that was lighter than air. The plane was born.

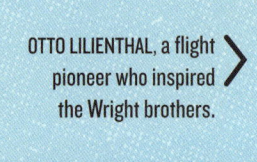

OTTO LILIENTHAL, a flight pioneer who inspired the Wright brothers.

THE WRIGHT FLYER

SOLAR IMPULSE 2

BOEING 747

Taking it further

Since the first flight of the *Wright Flyer* there have been countless aeroplane advances. These include:

- The jet engine allows planes to fly faster for longer. It was invented in 1937 and the first jet plane, the *Heinkel He 178*, was built two years later.

- Radar made it possible to detect planes far away and was first used in 1939.

- The first wide-bodied jet was the Boeing 747 Jumbo jet. From 1970 it made it easy to carry many passengers on long flights.

- *Solar Impulse 2* is powered by the Sun. In 2016 it flew 40,000 kilometres around the world without using a drop of fossil fuel. Solar panels across its 72-metre wingspan gather enough energy to carry the plane, which weighs about as much as a truck.

TRANSPORT AND VEHICLES

ROCKETS
The race to space

1926
American scientist Robert Goddard used liquid fuels – oxygen and gasoline – to launch a small rocket.

1957
Russia sent the first man-made satellite into space. *Sputnik* was the size of a beach ball and orbited the Earth about every 98 minutes.

1963
A geostationary satellite was launched that moved with the Earth so stayed fixed over the same spot on the planet. Today there are about 2,200 satellites orbiting our planet. They are vital for sending phone and TV signals, data for navigation systems via the Global Positioning System (GPS) and observing and measuring the weather.

1942
During World War 2, Germany developed the first long-range rocket: the V2 missile.

1961
Russian cosmonaut Yuri Gagarin become the first man in space, in a flight lasting 108 minutes. Two years later Valentina Tereshkova was the first woman to go into space, orbiting the Earth 48 times in 3 days.

1969
Neil Armstrong was the first man on the Moon (see page 60).

1977
The twin *Voyager 1* and *2* spacecraft were launched. They have sent back information and pictures about far-off planets and *Voyager 1* has now left our solar system and reached interstellar space.

1998
The International Space Station was launched. It is the biggest object ever flown in space and the first crew lived on it in 2000. It orbits the world every 90 minutes, travelling at 5 miles per second.

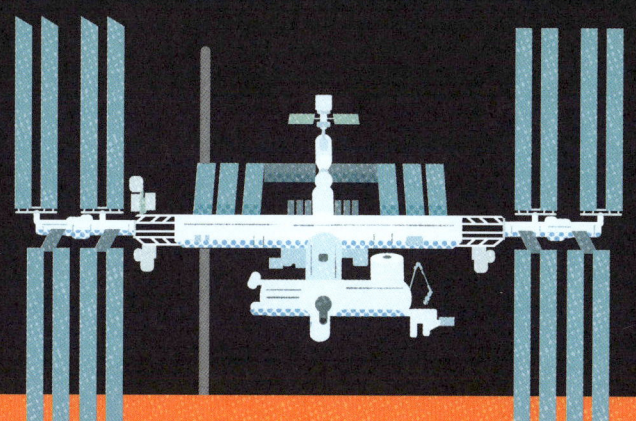

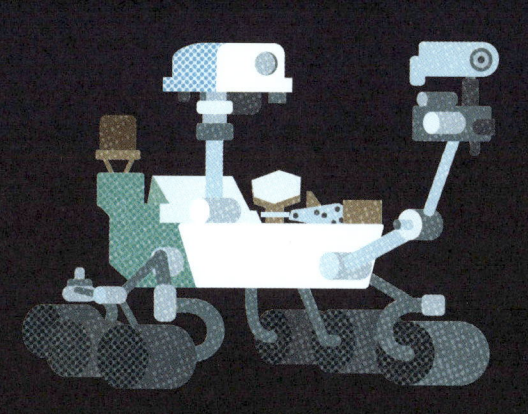

2012
The *Curiosity* Rover space probe landed on Mars. It is the largest and most advanced rover to land on the red planet.

The Chinese blasted fireworks into the sky many centuries ago, and used tubes to fire missiles in 1232 AD. But sending objects and people into space is one of our most recent achievements because it requires so much knowledge and energy.

1981
The *Columbia* Space shuttle launched. It was the first reusable spacecraft and flew 28 times before disaster struck when it blew up in 2003.

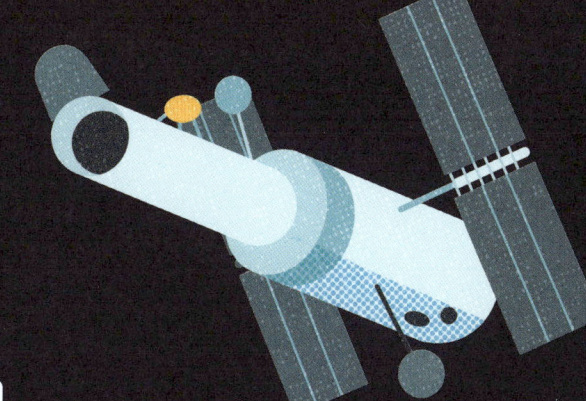

1990
The Hubble Space Telescope was launched. It is checked and repaired in space by astronauts, so that old instruments can be replaced.

TRANSPORT AND VEHICLES

APOLLO 11 THE RACE TO THE MOON

In July 1969, Neil Armstrong and Buzz Aldrin landed the *Eagle* lunar module and became the first humans to step onto another part of our universe.

Landing on the Moon is probably one of the greatest achievements of mankind. It took the latest technology, teamwork of about 400,000 people, and bravery and skill from the astronauts. Here is the story of what happened in the words of the people who were there.

On 25th May 1961, US President John F. Kennedy announced the plan for American astronauts to reach the Moon.

"I believe that this nation should commit itself to achieving the goal, before this decade is out, of landing a man on the Moon and returning him safely to the Earth."

On 16th July 1969, the Apollo 11 rocket took off carrying three astronauts, Neil Armstrong, Edwin "Buzz" Aldrin and Michael Collins. NASA's Jack King controlled the countdown from Johnson Space Center, Houston, Texas:

"Twelve, eleven, ten, nine, ignition sequence start. Six, five, four, three, two, one, zero, all engines running. Lift off! We have a lift off, 32 minutes past the hour. Lift off on Apollo 11."

Once Apollo 11 was in orbit, Armstrong and Aldrin climbed into the lunar module, called the *Eagle*. As the *Eagle* neared its landing site a warning light flashed.

"Program Alarm, it's a 1202."

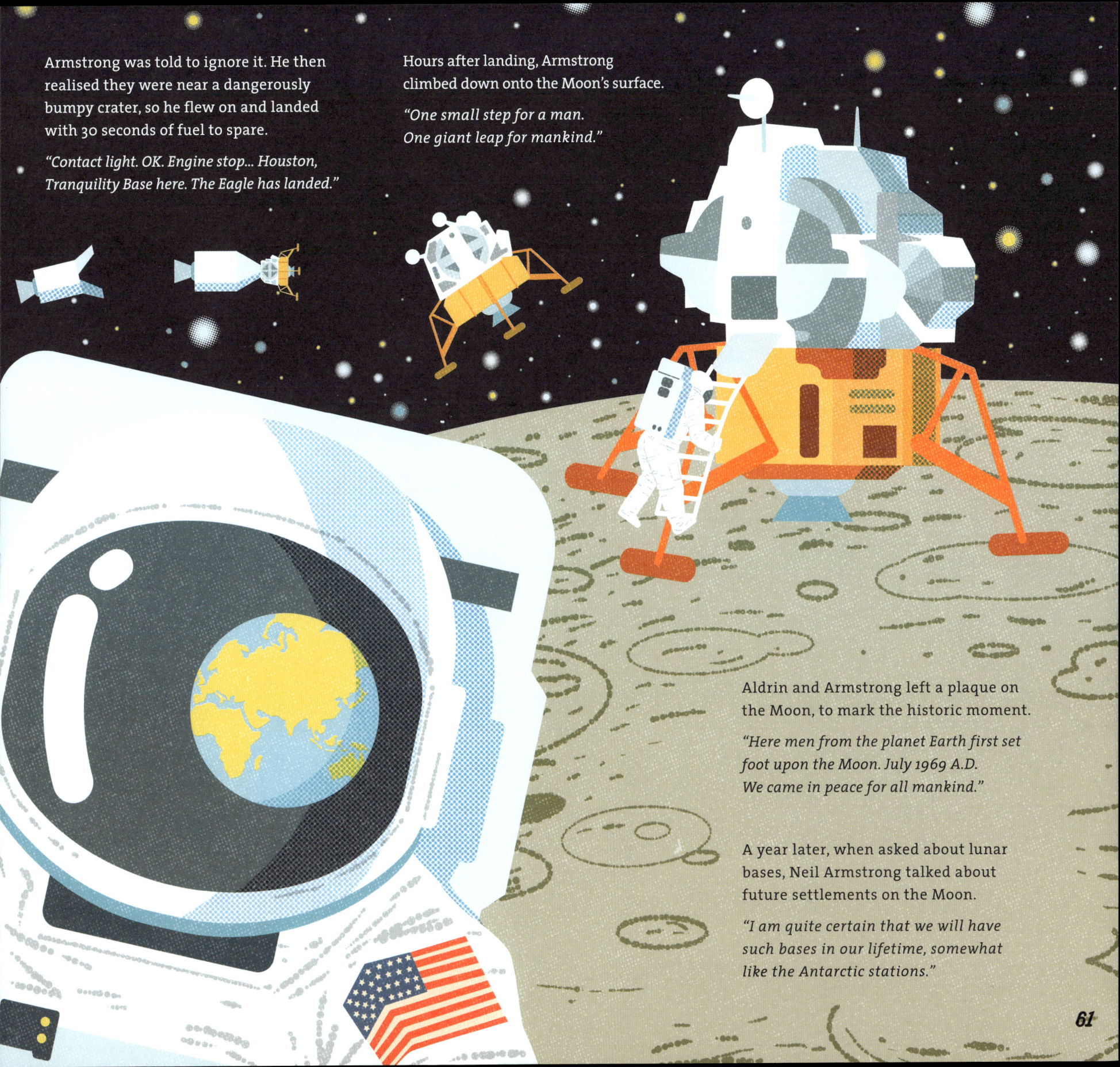

Armstrong was told to ignore it. He then realised they were near a dangerously bumpy crater, so he flew on and landed with 30 seconds of fuel to spare.

"Contact light. OK. Engine stop... Houston, Tranquility Base here. The Eagle has landed."

Hours after landing, Armstrong climbed down onto the Moon's surface.

"One small step for a man. One giant leap for mankind."

Aldrin and Armstrong left a plaque on the Moon, to mark the historic moment.

"Here men from the planet Earth first set foot upon the Moon. July 1969 A.D. We came in peace for all mankind."

A year later, when asked about lunar bases, Neil Armstrong talked about future settlements on the Moon.

"I am quite certain that we will have such bases in our lifetime, somewhat like the Antarctic stations."

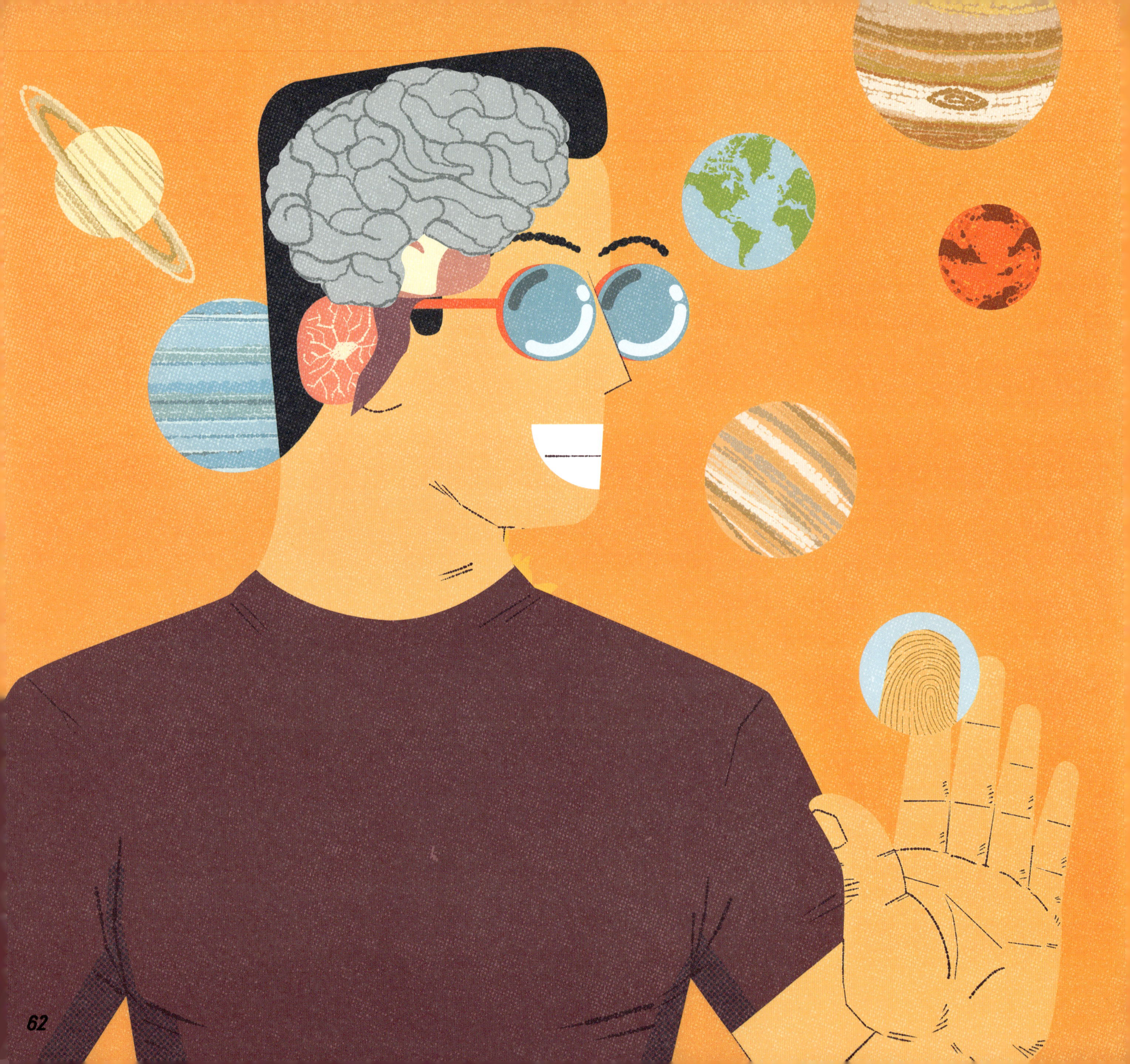

SCIENCE AND OUR WORLD

Why can't we fly? What makes us ill? How does the world work? Find out how brilliant individuals or teams of scientists have developed areas of medicine, physics, biology and astronomy to show us how the world works.

SCIENCE AND OUR WORLD

STAYING ALIVE! THE RACE AGAINST DISEASE

For thousands of years, people did not know what caused illnesses. A disease called the plague killed millions of people across Europe in the 14th century because none of the suggested cures worked. But these four medical achievements have saved millions of lives.

PLAGUE MASK
beak filled with herbs, aimed to protect doctors from the plague in the mid-1300s

New treatment

Smallpox was a deadly disease that killed a tenth of all the children in Britain in the 18th century. Edward Jenner heard a dairymaid say that she would not get it after she survived the milder illness called cowpox. In 1796, Jenner scratched cowpox puss onto the skin of a boy called James Phipps, waited, then rubbed in smallpox pus. This could have been dangerous, but the method worked and James did not get the disease. Edward called the treatment 'vaccination'. It took a while for people to accept the idea, but doctors began to vaccinate against many diseases – including plague, in 1897.

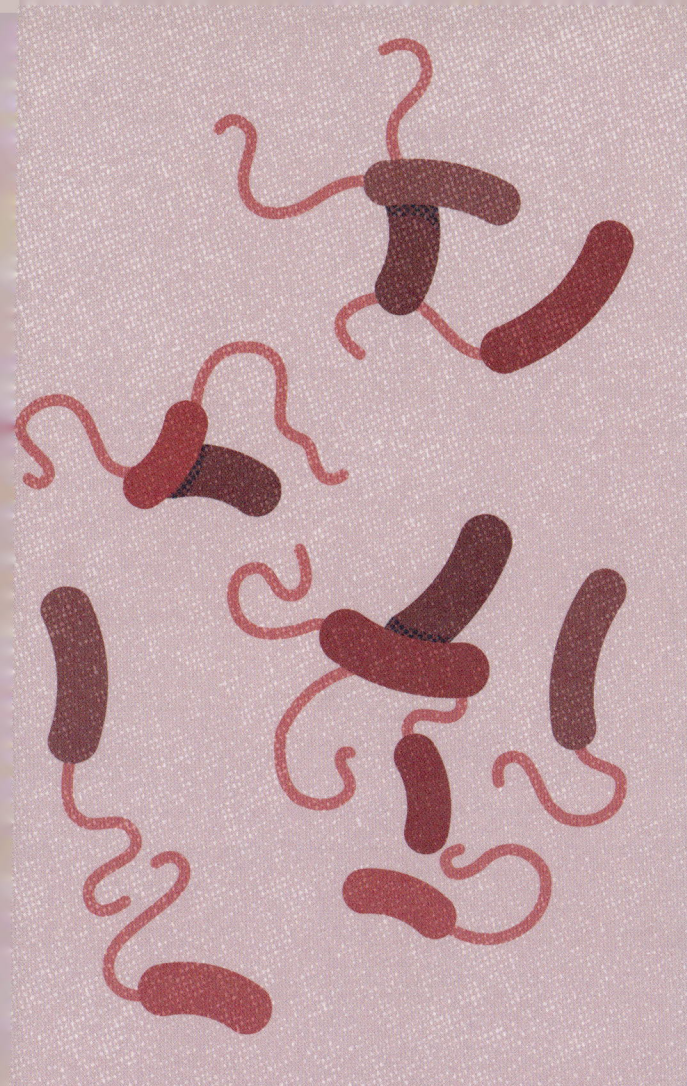

Safer operations

In the 1860s Joseph Lister noted that many patients died not during but after operations, where they had been cut open by a surgeon. He used Pasteur's ideas on germs to set out rules that we take for granted today:

- Surgeons wash before each operation
- Instruments are sterilised (made germ-free)
- Operating rooms are very clean
- Wounds are covered with bandages soaked in mild acid to kill germs

He was right and is known as 'the father of antiseptic surgery'.

What are germs?

Cholera was a very dangerous disease in the 19th century, killing sufferers very quickly. Most people thought illnesses came from 'bad air', so many treatments used herbs and flowers to make a nice smell. But in 1854 John Snow used a map to show that many people with the disease drank dirty water from the same pump. When he removed the pump handle, the number of cholera victims fell. Snow's work, together with the work of others, helped Louis Pasteur show that tiny organisms called microbes (germs) cause diseases, in 1861.

Antibiotics

In 1928, Alexander Fleming noticed a furry growth on a dish where he was growing bacteria (tiny living organisms). He could have thrown this mould out, but he realised that it was killing the bacteria. He called it 'penicillin', and a decade later, Howard Florey and Ernst Chain worked out how to make enough of it to treat lots of people and save many lives during World War 2 (1939-1945). The discovery led to the use of medicines now known as antibiotics that treat diseases caused by bacteria.

SCIENCE AND OUR WORLD

CHARLES DARWIN THE RACE TO EVOLVE

We know that humans are a type of ape and have adapted and changed over many thousands of years. Yet if you'd suggested it 200 years ago, people would have thought you were mad. Charles Darwin was very important in our understanding of our origins.

Darwin was born in Shrewsbury, England in 1809. His mother died when he was eight and his sisters helped to bring him up. He didn't like school much, and went on to study religion, although he was also very interested in plants and animals.

In 1831 he sailed on the *HMS Beagle* as it set off to study the coast of South America. The journey lasted for 5 years and included many long stays on land – which was just as well, because Darwin got very seasick. Their stop-offs included Brazil, Australia and the Galapagos Islands in the Pacific Ocean.

Darwin studied not just the plants and animals but the rocks and fossils he found. He saw that:

- There were many fossils of animals that were extinct.
- Earth was much older than the Bible said.
- There were many different types of the same animal, for example lots of similar birds with differently shaped beaks.

66

PAST

PRESENT

New ideas

It took 20 years for Darwin to think through and write his new ideas. At this time many people believed the story in the Bible about how God made the world and its creatures. Others believed that living things changed over time, taking features and behaviours from their parents but sometimes with small, new changes. In 1859, Darwin published a book that said:

- Many different living things come from the same beginning.
- Animals and plants do not stay the same but adapt over time to suit their habitat.
- Weaker animals who fail to change in this way will die out.

In later versions of the book, he used the phrase 'survival of the fittest'. His key idea became known as natural selection, and is still taught today.

SCIENCE AND OUR WORLD

FIX ME! THE RACE TO CURE

The Ancient Egyptians mummified dead bodies by drying them out, stuffing them and wrapping them in bandages. They also took out the insides of the dead and stored them in jars. They kept major organs such as the heart, but threw away the brain because they did not think it was important! Here are some of the achievements, from the ancient world to the modern day, in understanding and fixing our bodies.

BRAIN
Ancient people did brain surgery. This included trepanning (drilling a hole in the skull) which sometimes worked! Harvey Cushing was the first modern brain surgeon. In 1908 he removed harmful growths from inside a skull.

SPECTACLES
The first spectacles were probably made in the 13th century in Italy, which had excellent glass making skills. Contact lenses were first fitted in 1887.

TEETH
From 1851 false teeth could be set into a rubber base that fitted over the gums. This was invented by Charles Goodyear, still famous for rubber tyres.

HEARING AIDS
The first known hearing aids were funnel-shaped 'ear trumpets' sold from 1800. Today's tiny hearing aids are digital and powered by tiny rechargeable batteries.

HEART
In 1628, William Harvey showed how the heart pumps blood round the body and that veins have one-way valves to stop blood flowing backwards. The first 'artificial pacemaker' device for keeping the heart going was invented in 1932. The first heart transplant operation took place in 1967.

KIDNEYS
Kidneys filter waste from our blood. Kidney transplants had failed until US surgeon Joseph Murray realised that the body's immune system rejected them. In 1954 he succeeded by operating on identical twins. From the early 1960s drugs were developed to deal with the immune system problem.

HANDS
In 1579, Ambroise Pare wrote how he had made and fitted an artificial hand that had a hinge to move better. He also made prosthetic arms and legs.

HIPS
In 1891, Themistocles Gluck replaced a patient's hip with a new, artificial joint made from ivory.

KNEES
Knee replacement surgery was first performed in the 1950s.

FINGERPRINTS
It was already known that each of us has our own fingerprint pattern when, in 1892, Argentinian police officer Juan Vucetich used them as evidence in a murder case.

BLOOD
The ancient Greeks knew something of the difference between arteries (which carry oxygen-rich blood from the heart) and veins (which return it to the heart) from about 500BC. From 1902 we knew people have four main blood groups. This made blood transfusions, which were already happening, more successful.

SCIENCE AND OUR WORLD

THE BODY — THE RACE TO SEE INSIDE

Being able to see inside our bodies without cutting them open has helped keep a lot of people alive and healthy. Besides being important in medicine, these various technologies are also valuable in other areas.

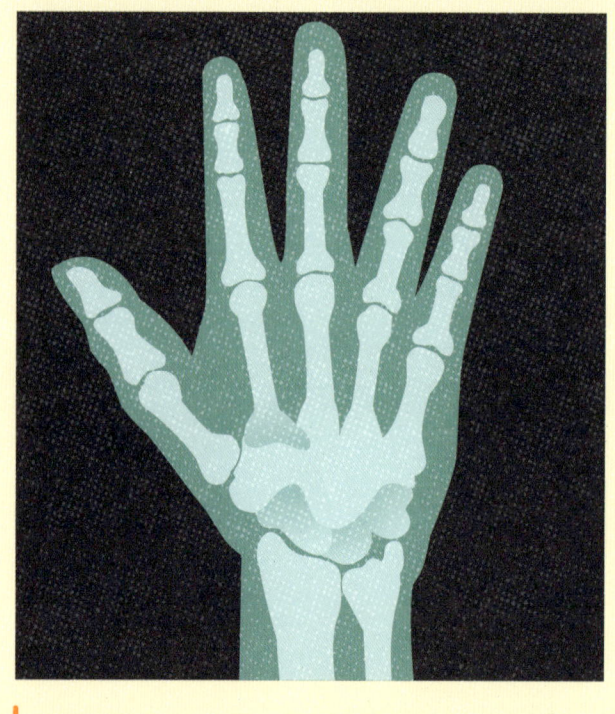

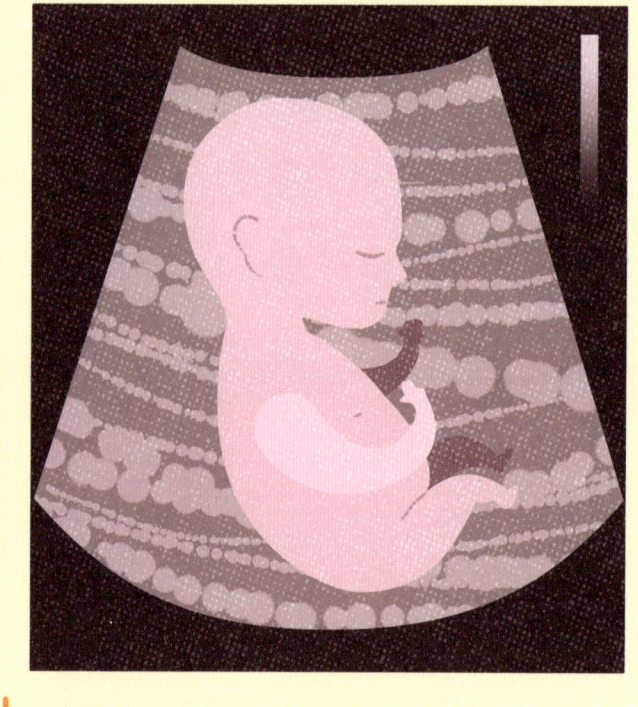

Images made by:	**X-RAYS.** These invisible rays pass through soft materials but not harder things such as bone. They can be very harmful in large amounts.	**ULTRASOUND.** This measures how long sound waves take to bounce back or travel through something.
Discovered by:	Wilhelm Röntgen in 1895. He found them by accident when he was studying how electrical rays go through gases.	Dr Ian Donald used the existing knowledge about sounds to try ultrasound medically from 1956.
Use:	Seeing bones and other solid objects inside our bodies.	Breaking of kidney stones inside our bodies and seeing inside pregnant stomachs to check babies.
Some non-medical uses:	Looking inside baggage at airports, scanning cargo loads, looking at outer space and seeing under layers of paint in old pictures.	Checking for faults and cracks in structures such as bridges. Sound waves can also be used underwater to spot objects and to measure depth, and bats use them to sense in the dark!

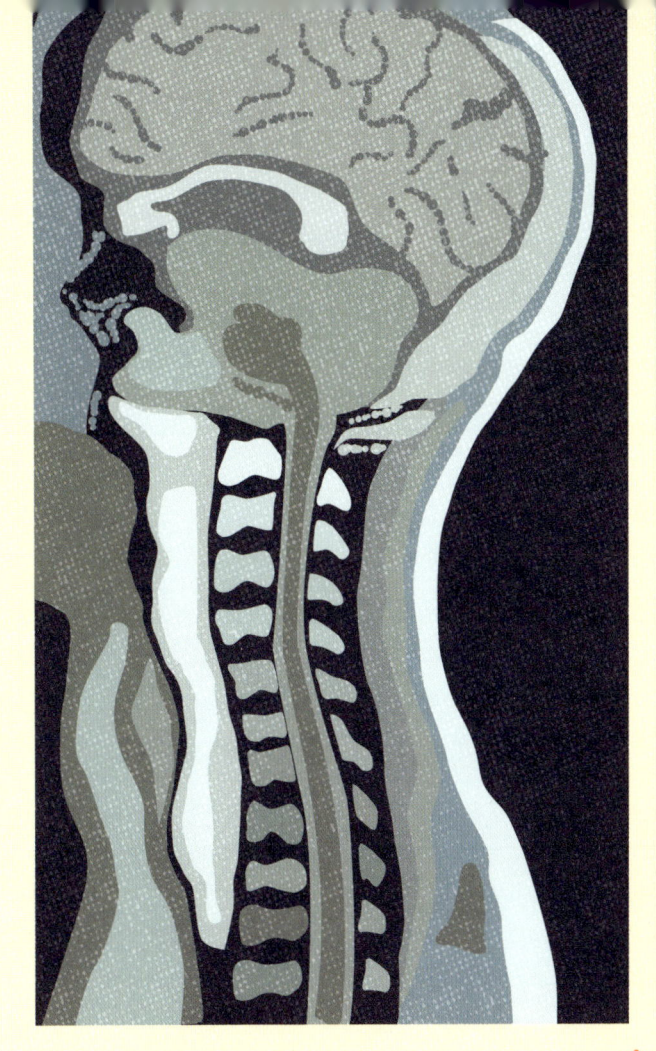

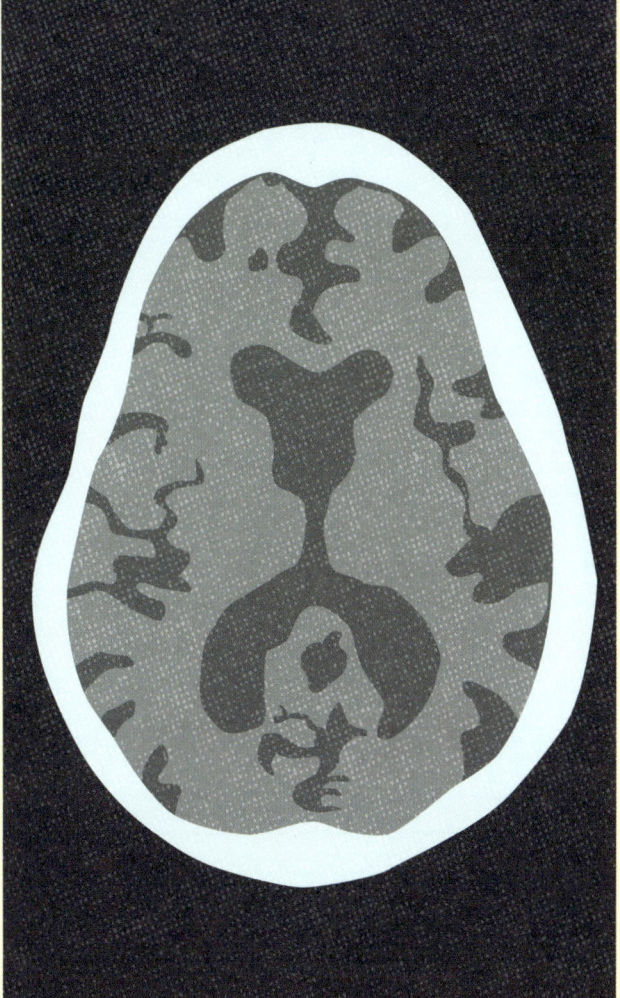

MRI (MAGNETIC RESONANCE IMAGING). This works by sending harmless radio waves through a magnetic field.

Various scientists and doctors, including Paul Lauterbur, Peter Mansfield and Raymond Damadian. It was first used in 1972.	Engineer Godfrey Hounsfield and physicist Allan Cormack developed it in 1972.
Showing how joints work and spotting extra growths inside a body.	First developed to look inside the brain, and now used elsewhere in the body.
Analysing chemicals and checking water and fat content in foods.	Spotting flaws in machine parts, finding minerals in mining and detecting explosives.

CT SCANS. Combines many X-ray images to create a 3D image, a bit like bread slices in a loaf.

Understanding ourselves

In the 1950s British scientist Rosalind Franklin used X-rays to show the basic shape/structure of the DNA molecule. This helped American James Watson and Briton Francis Crick to identify DNA that carries all the instructions our cells need for us to live. This major discovery has medical uses, and is also valuable in criminal cases as we leave traces of our DNA everywhere we go.

SCIENCE AND OUR WORLD

MARIE CURIE THE RADIATION RACE

Marie Curie was the first woman to be accepted as a scientist and to receive a Nobel Prize, a big international award (in fact she won two, for physics and chemistry). Her work on radiation saved lives – but eventually killed her.

Marie was born in Poland in 1867. Her sister and then her mother died when she was young, which made her lose her faith in God. Instead she turned to science. She loved studying but women were not allowed to go to university where she lived, so she saved hard to pay to go to one in Paris, France in 1891. Around this time Wilhelm Röntgen discovered X-rays (see page 70) and Henri Becquerel realised that uranium released similar but different rays. Marie and her new husband Pierre decided to investigate.

RA 88

During her career, Curie made important discoveries, including:

- Showing that atoms are not the smallest form of matter.
- Discovering two new elements.
- Discovering that radium could treat an illness called cancer.
- She made a mobile X-ray unit used during World War 1 (1914-18).

Marie and Pierre spent years testing powders of a strange, rare rock called pitchblende. It was hard work. "Sometimes I had to spend a whole day stirring a boiling mass with a heavy iron rod nearly as big as myself," Marie wrote.

But it paid off when the tons of powdered rock produced a few traces of a new element that she named 'polonium', after her home country of Poland.

Pierre tragically died when he was hit by a horse and cart in 1906, but Marie carried on the work, and in 1910 produced a tiny amount of a new silver-white metal called radium. But no one knew that large amounts of radioactivity harm our bodies. Eventually this and her work with X-rays killed Marie Curie in 1934. Her notebooks are still so dangerously radioactive that they are kept in protective lead-lined boxes.

Building blocks

Elements are the basic blocks that everything – you, Earth, the Universe – is made from. Marie discovered elements to add to the periodic table. The table is a way of showing how different elements behave and are related to each other. It was devised by Dmitri Mendeleev in 1869. He got the idea from a game where cards are placed in rows and columns. He left gaps where new elements could be added. Marie Curie filled in some of those spaces.

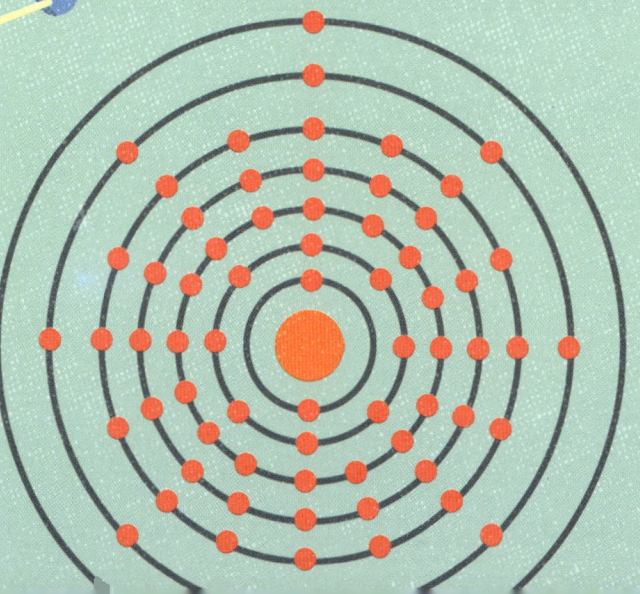

SCIENCE AND OUR WORLD

LOOKING UP THE RACE TO KNOW THE STARS

People have marvelled at the night sky for many thousands of years. Careful observation revealed patterns. The Stonehenge stone circle is one example of early structures built to line up with the rising Sun. People assumed that the stars swirl around us in the middle of our universe. We now know that isn't true.

The Sun is a star

Some Ancient Greeks thought the Sun was a star, but the idea didn't catch on. In 1543, Nicolaus Copernicus suggested that the Earth and other planets circle around the Sun, a revolutionary idea at the time. About 50 years later, Italian Giordano Bruno said he thought the Sun is a star, but he was burned alive as a punishment! We now know that Copernicus and Bruno were right. The Sun is a star and all the planets in our solar system orbit around it.

There are other planets

MARS Early civilisations saw Mars as a bright light different to the stars. In 1609, Johannes Kepler showed that its orbit was not a perfect circle – an astounding idea for the time.

VENUS The earliest writing about Venus dates from about 1600BC. In 1610 Galileo Galilei noticed that it changes shape, like the Moon, and orbits the Sun.

MERCURY Assyrian writings from about 1000BC called Mercury "the jumping planet". Later, the Romans named it after their messenger god as it moves across the sky so fast.

SATURN & JUPITER Around 700BC the Assyrians wrote about Saturn and Jupiter. Galileo saw Saturn's rings through his telescope, but the image was so poor he thought they might be moons... or ears! He was first to notice Saturn's four moons.

URANUS William Herschel discovered the planet Uranus in 1781, although he thought it was a comet.

NEPTUNE John Couch Adams first identified the gas giant, Neptune, in 1846.

PLUTO In 1930, Clyde Tombaugh used observation and calculation to find Pluto. It turned out his sums were wrong, but he still found it! Pluto was moved down the rankings to a dwarf planet in 2006.

There are other galaxies

In 1929 Edwin Hubble published his calculations showing that many stars lie far beyond the Milky Way. Now we know there are other galaxies apart from our own.

Our universe began with the Big Bang

In 1965, astronomers Arno Penzias and Robert Wilson were puzzled by a strange hiss coming from outer space. They cleaned and checked their equipment looking for a flaw before they realised it was a sound from far back in time: the Big Bang that created our universe.

SCIENCE AND OUR WORLD

ISAAC NEWTON
THE RACE TO UNDERSTAND GRAVITY

Isaac Newton was a great scientist who helped us understand our world. When he was born in 1642, his father had already died, and soon his mother sent him to live with his grandparents in their house by an orchard. Isaac was clever and inventive: he made a mouse-powered windmill, he loved flying kites with lanterns tied onto their strings and he taught himself a lot about science.

By the 15th century, astronomers knew that the Earth spins and that planets revolve around the Sun. But they didn't understand why we don't fall off, or how the orbits keep going. One day, an apple falling from a tree in the orchard made Isaac wonder why it fell straight down and not in a curve or even sideways. He realised that an invisible force was at work on the apple, on everything on Earth, and on the planets in space.

Newton called this force 'gravity', from the Latin word for 'weight', and in 1687 he wrote a set of laws about forces that show:

- Objects move in the direction they are pushed, and keep going in a straight line until something slows or deflects them.
- Force overcomes inertia and causes acceleration.
- When a force pushes one way, an equal force always pushes in the opposite direction. This is called an equal and opposite reaction.

Suddenly the universe made more sense.

Newton also studied light and showed that rainbows form when white light is scattered into separate colours. He also built a telescope that used mirrors instead of lenses. This gave much better results, and today's huge telescopes still use this method.

More gravity

Albert Einstein (1879-1955) was another original thinker who taught himself science. He took Newton's work many steps further, showing that Newton's laws work well until we reach the speed of light. This and other studies helped scientists to understand our universe better and led to the development of nuclear power.

Black holes

In 1783, English scientist John Michell suggested that Newton's writings showed there could be objects with such strong gravity that not even light could escape their gravitational pull. Einstein's work backed this up, and the first 'black hole' was spotted in 1971 by British astronomers Louise Webster and Paul Murdin.

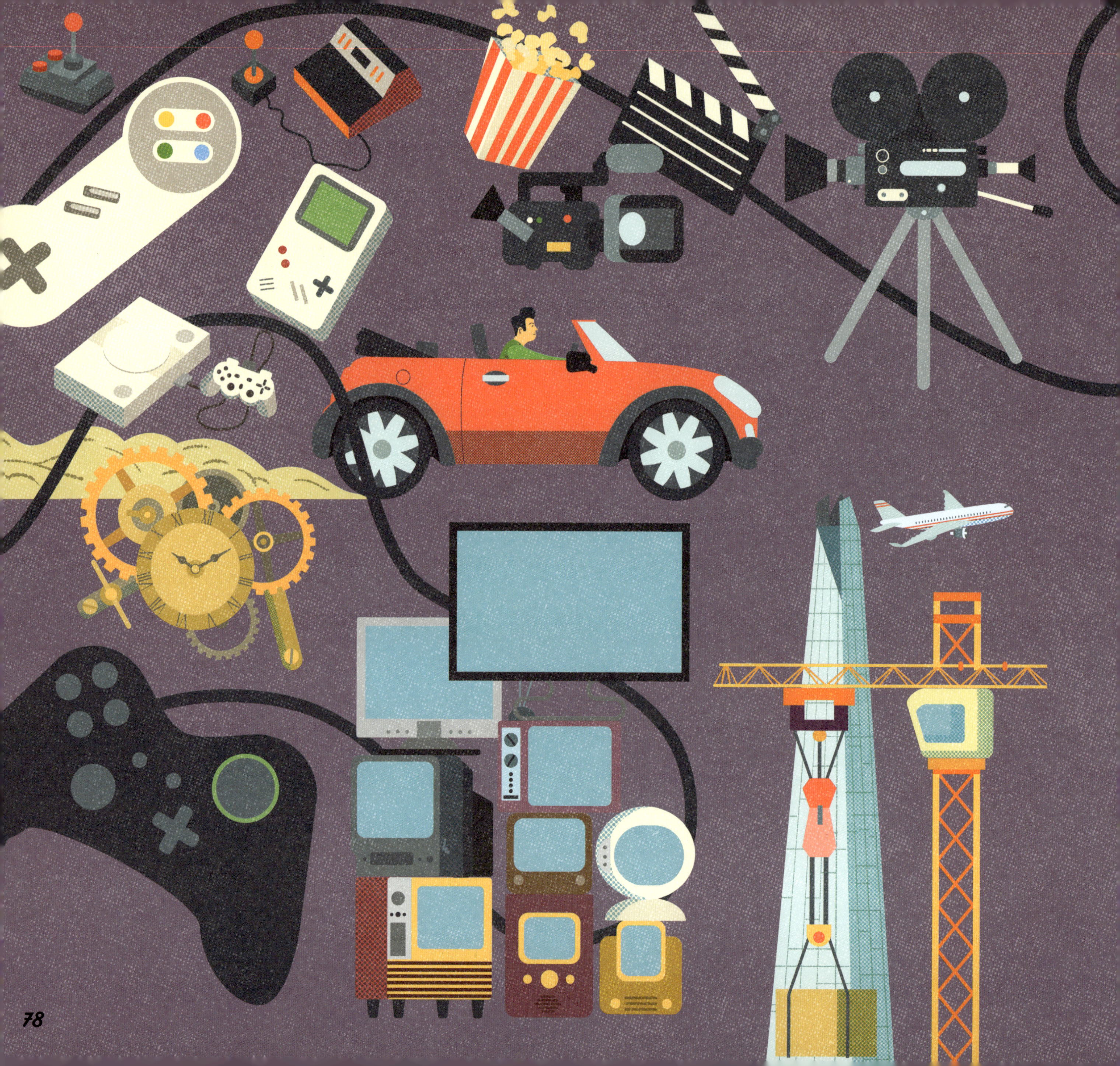

TECHNOLOGY

Humans have valued tools since we first sharpened rocks into blades and added a handle to make an axe. Technology has changed our world, allowing instant communication, helping grow more food and making lives better in countless ways. Learn how many inventions evolved from something that came before.

TECHNOLOGY

THE SPARK
The race for electricity

1600
English doctor and scientist William Gilbert first used the word 'electricus' in his writings on magnetism and static electricity. He based it on the Greek word for amber – fossilised tree resin that the ancient Greeks rubbed with fur to make static electricity.

1786
Italian biologist Luigi Galvani made a dead frog's legs twitch by touching them with two metals. He thought electricity was from inside the frog's body.

1821
French scientist André-Marie Ampère showed that electricity and magnetism work together to make a force. Electrical current is measured in amps.

1752
American Benjamin Franklin supposedly flew a kite in a thunderstorm with a metal key tied to its wet string. Sparks jumped from the key to his hand to prove that lightning was electricity. He was lucky he wasn't killed!

1800
Alessandro Volta realised his friend Galvani's metals had created an electrical current. He then invented a battery to store electricity. The 'push' that moves charged electrons (current) along a circuit is measured in volts, from his name.

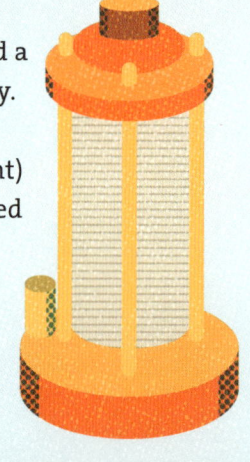

1821
Englishman Michael Faraday made the first simple electric motor. He created a generator ten years later and showed that a magnetic field could produce electricity.

1877
Thomas Doolittle of America found a way to make strong, thin copper wire that was used to connect telegraphs (see page 88), and later, telephones.

1882
Edison designed the first electric power station in New York.

1897
British scientist Sir Joseph John Thomson showed that electrons can move between atoms. This flow is the electrical current that transfers energy along a conductor: now we knew how electricity works.

One of the human race's great achievements is producing electricity to make light and power. It is impossible to imagine our world without it, but it took many steps to get there…

1879
Thomas Edison in America and Joseph Swan in Britain both created light bulbs, in which electric current heated thin wire until it glowed and emitted light. Now homes could be lit well and safely – previously people had relied on candles, whale oil and gas, which were all smelly, smoky and dangerous.

1893
Nikola Tesla developed alternating current (AC), a safe, reliable system still used to deliver our electric power today.

1898
From here on a huge range of machines for the home were invented, including washing machines, dishwashers, fridges and ovens. Shops were now brightly lit, and in 1898 the first electric escalator whirred into action in London store Harrods. The electric age began.

TECHNOLOGY
WHEELS: A TURNING POINT

The wheel is probably our most important invention. It allowed people to haul heavy things from early times and is as vital to our lives today – nearly every machine has wheels on or inside it.

Rolling story
Pot makers around 3500BC used a turning wheel to help shape clay into bowls. This may be where the idea for the transport wheel came from, or perhaps it was from moving heavy objects by rolling them on tree trunks.

Soon, humans were using carts to carry heavy or bulky things, and chariots for fighting faster over greater distances. Early wheels were solid, but they got lighter after spokes were invented. From about 500BC metal rims wrapped around the wood made wheels stronger. In the 19th century, air-filled rubber tires made rides smoother.

Water power
Water wheels used the power of flowing rivers from the 1st century BC. This was an alternative to people or animals using their arms or legs to power machines.

Wheel cloth

Humans turned fibres into thread with spinning wheels from about 500AD. The device was vital for making yarn or thread for cloth over many centuries. From 1764, a machine called the spinning jenny did the work of eight spinning wheels at once, to produce thread far more quickly.

Pulling wheels

Running a rope around a wheel makes a pulley – a machine for lifting and lowering things such as ship sails. Today, they turn airplane rudders and are how cranes lift materials to build skyscrapers.

Counting wheels

Put raised teeth around a wheel and you can transfer energy as it spins. This is called a cog and is how many machines and gears work. An early example of working cogs is found in mechanical clocks that first ticked in the 14th century. Until then, people measured time by the Sun's position, or by using water or sand timers.

83

TECHNOLOGY
COMPUTERS THE DATA RACE

Creating computers and connecting them around the world is one of the great human achievements. It took many small steps, including making tiny 'chips' with vast memory stores. Computers are part of our everyday lives, from playing games to running factories.

The first computers were huge and not very powerful. By the 1980s small personal computers (PCs) could be used at home.

In 1801 Frenchman JOSEPH-MARIE JACQUARD invented a weaving machine that used punched wooden cards. This was how early computers worked.

THE ABACUS counting frame was an early calculating machine still used today.

In 1832 CHARLES BABBAGE designed a machine to do complicated sums. If he had raised the money to build it, it would have been the first computer. Ada Lovelace then created the punch cards that could work with his Analytical Engine – making her the first computer programmer!

2007 saw the first SMARTPHONE that put many features of a computer onto a small screen. Tablets followed three years later.

Why QWERTY?

Computer keyboards are set in a letter pattern taken from typewriters. Typewriters appeared from 1874 to allow people to write faster than with a pen. The letter layout is known as 'QWERTY' from its top line and was thought to prevent the machine jamming, as people couldn't type as fast.

In 1969, the American government found a way to connect its computers together – the FIRST NETWORK. The Internet is today's term for our worldwide computer network.

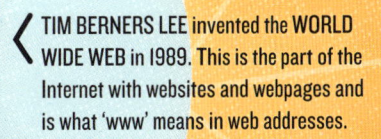

TIM BERNERS LEE invented the WORLD WIDE WEB in 1989. This is the part of the Internet with websites and webpages and is what 'www' means in web addresses.

The idea for a TOUCHSCREEN had been around for a while before the first finger swipe instruction was given in 1977.

During World War 2 (1939-45) ALAN TURING created machines to break secret enemy codes.

85

TECHNOLOGY

POWER! THE RACE FOR ENERGY

Early people used fuel for warmth and light. As we invented devices to do work for us, we tied animals to them to turn wheels, and later found fuels to power our machinery. Climate change is pushing us to switch to renewable and less harmful sources of energy.

Fire!

Early fuels included straw, dung, peat (decayed plant matter) and wood. Then we learned to dig down for coal that burned at hotter temperatures – excellent for powering steam engines. Coal was our most important fuel from 1850-1945 and was also burned as a gas. Oil power came after the first oil well was drilled in 1859 in Pennsylvania, USA. As well as being a fuel, oil is where our plastics come from. Recently, we have gone back to burning plant material, manure and other organic matter as fuel instead, because these are renewable sources of energy. We call these biomass fuels.

Water

Water was once as important a power source as oil is to us today. Fast flowing water turned wheels, so we built mills next to rivers to grind grain for flour. Damming rivers to control the flow led to the development of the hydroelectric dam, where spinning turbines generated electricity. The first was built in 1882 in Wisconsin, America. We now also get power from the movement of the waves and tides.

Wind

There may have been windmills in Persia as early as the 7th century, and the idea first reached England in the 12th century. Machinery for grinding was put in fields rather than by rivers. Today, wind farms generate electricity by turning turbines.

Nuclear

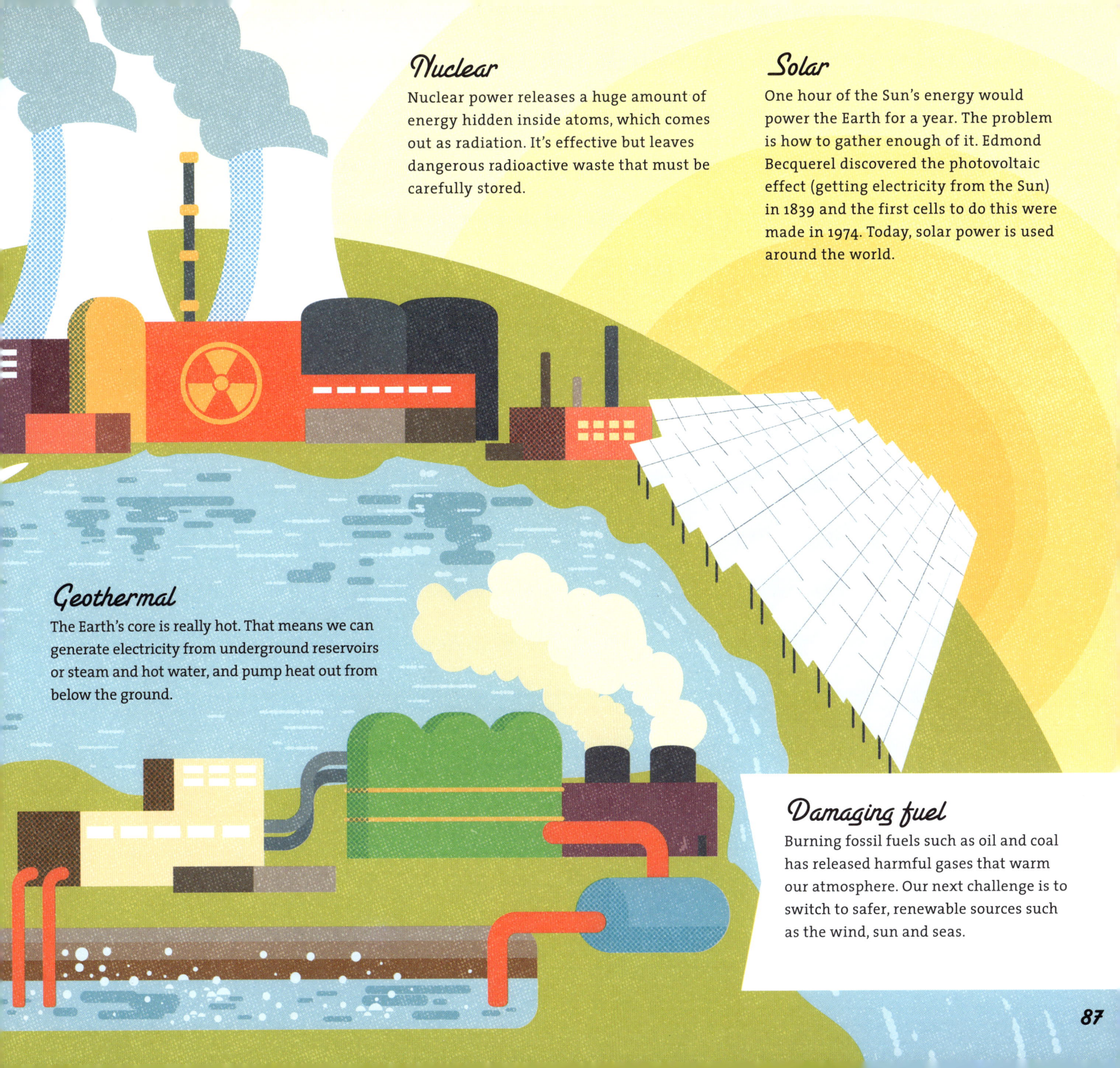

Nuclear power releases a huge amount of energy hidden inside atoms, which comes out as radiation. It's effective but leaves dangerous radioactive waste that must be carefully stored.

Solar

One hour of the Sun's energy would power the Earth for a year. The problem is how to gather enough of it. Edmond Becquerel discovered the photovoltaic effect (getting electricity from the Sun) in 1839 and the first cells to do this were made in 1974. Today, solar power is used around the world.

Geothermal

The Earth's core is really hot. That means we can generate electricity from underground reservoirs or steam and hot water, and pump heat out from below the ground.

Damaging fuel

Burning fossil fuels such as oil and coal has released harmful gases that warm our atmosphere. Our next challenge is to switch to safer, renewable sources such as the wind, sun and seas.

TECHNOLOGY

3200 BC WRITING
The first writing was on wet clay, followed by a kind of paper called papyrus from about 2500 BC. People also wrote on wax, stone and animal skin or plant fibre. Armies developed codes so that messages could be kept secret even if the enemy got hold of them.

1448 PRINTING
Books were hand painted until the invention of the Gutenberg printing press. For the first time, large numbers of the same book could be produced. However, most people were still unable to read and write, so it was mainly the rich and educated who could communicate best through printed material.

1837 THE TELEGRAPH
The telegraph was the next big advance because messages could be sent a long way very quickly. It needed electricity and a network of wires on poles. Telegraph operators tapped out dots and dashes using the Morse Code system.

COMMUNICATION
From smoke signals to SMS

1150 CARRIER PIGEONS
Pigeons were trained to fly long distances carrying messages tied to their legs.

1635 POSTAL SERVICE
In the 17th century, postal services began to carry letters, often via messengers on horseback. This later led to the use of stamps to pay the carrier.

1876 THE TELEPHONE
The telephone first allowed people to chat even when they were far apart. The phones were linked by a network of wires, which later became known as landlines.

1895 RADIO

Radio allowed sounds and messages to travel very long distances. The system was sometimes called 'the wireless' because the signal travelled through the air and not along cables. Companies were set up to broadcast programmes.

1983 MOBILE PHONES

Early mobile phones were about the size and weight of a brick! They have become an essential piece of communications equipment with uses far beyond speaking directly to other people, which was their original job. The first text message was sent in 1992.

The race to communicate better has lasted as long as people have. We love talking to each other! Early communication methods included smoke signals, fire, drums and cave paintings, but the use of electricity, radio waves and satellites along with other technologies has allowed us to send and receive better quality messages faster and faster.

1927 TELEVISION

The invention of television added pictures to the mix. Space technology such as satellites (1957) meant the images could be bounced through the atmosphere. At first the images were only black and white and they could be quite fuzzy. Colour images (1953) were a big improvement.

1990 THE INTERNET

At first, the global computer network, called the Internet, was a dial-up service delivered via the phone line. Today the links are by cable, fibre or wireless via satellite and are used for things such as electronic mail, online chat, sharing documents, downloading movies, playing games and reading pages on the World Wide Web.

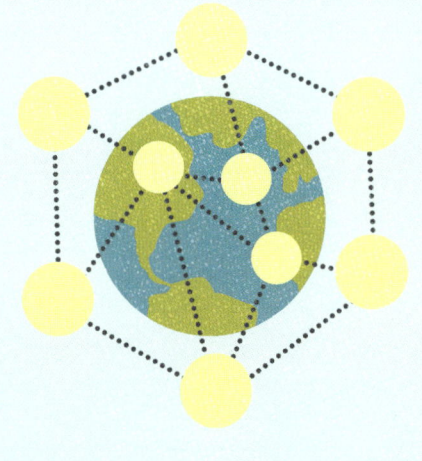

TECHNOLOGY

MEDIA THE RACE TO BE ENTERTAINED

In Ancient Egypt, over 5000 years ago, children played games with round stones that we would now call marbles. A few centuries later, their descendants slid ivory or stone pieces across a sheet in one of the earliest board games, called senet. Here are some more recent ways we have found to entertain ourselves.

Long waves

Heinrich Hertz proved the existence of radio waves in 1888 and eight years later Guglielmo Marconi sent messages without wires. In 1901 he broadcast a message across the Atlantic Ocean and radio really took off. It was particularly valuable to ships in trouble at sea as they could now ask for help from a long way off, out of sight.

Hear hear!

The first recording devices used wax-coated wire until Emile Berliner switched to metal discs on his gramophone in 1887. Later, music playing advanced to long-playing vinyl records, which first spun in 1948, then cassette tapes which whirred from 1962. Compact discs (CDs) reached the shops in 1982, and then finally, from 1998, digital music devices allowed users to download music from the Internet.

Movie story

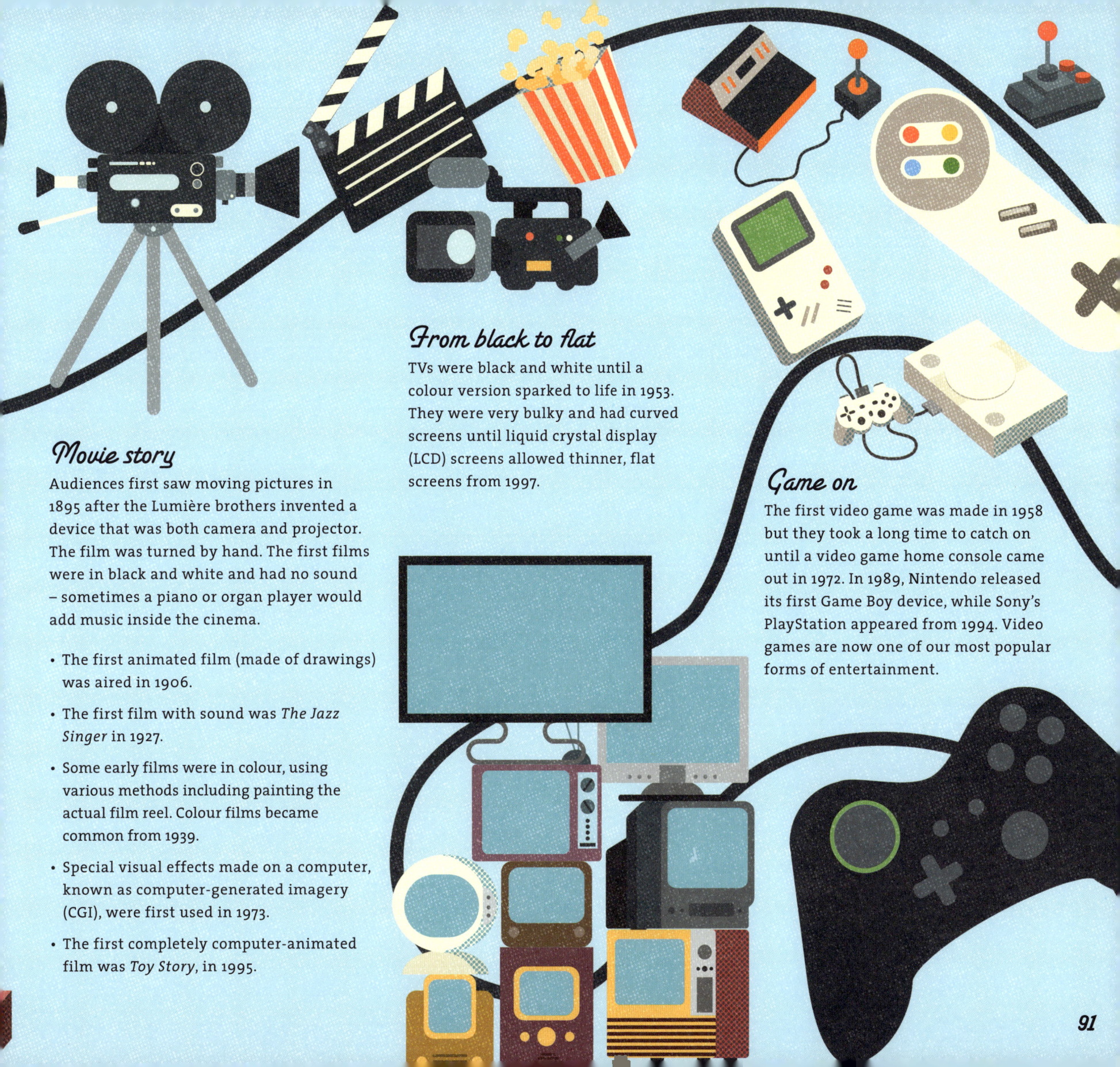

Audiences first saw moving pictures in 1895 after the Lumière brothers invented a device that was both camera and projector. The film was turned by hand. The first films were in black and white and had no sound – sometimes a piano or organ player would add music inside the cinema.

- The first animated film (made of drawings) was aired in 1906.
- The first film with sound was *The Jazz Singer* in 1927.
- Some early films were in colour, using various methods including painting the actual film reel. Colour films became common from 1939.
- Special visual effects made on a computer, known as computer-generated imagery (CGI), were first used in 1973.
- The first completely computer-animated film was *Toy Story*, in 1995.

From black to flat

TVs were black and white until a colour version sparked to life in 1953. They were very bulky and had curved screens until liquid crystal display (LCD) screens allowed thinner, flat screens from 1997.

Game on

The first video game was made in 1958 but they took a long time to catch on until a video game home console came out in 1972. In 1989, Nintendo released its first Game Boy device, while Sony's PlayStation appeared from 1994. Video games are now one of our most popular forms of entertainment.

TECHNOLOGY
FARMING THE RACE TO GROW FOOD

Feeding a growing population requires a lot of work. Farming has changed the landscape of our world, and the food it supplies has allowed us to develop civilisations and build cities.

From hunting to building

Early people fished, hunted animals and gathered food from wild plants, so they moved about a lot more than we do today. Roughly 12,000 years ago we started to grow crops such as wheat and keep animals like goats, so people built houses to stay near their fields and protect them. Settlements grew. The first city is thought to be Uruk from about 4500 BC in what is now Iraq.

Less toil on the soil

A plough turns soil over ready for planting, improving drainage and burying weeds. Before ploughs, farmers had to turn over their soil with a spade, which was slow, tough work. The first plough was basically a thick, sharpened stick pulled by people, but soon farmers trained animals to pull the plough along. The next improvements were adding blades to cut into the soil, and adding wheels to help travel over rough ground. Modern mechanical ploughs work much faster. They have rows of blades, that are tilted to turn over the soil quickly and easily.

Water works

Crops need water, and people have found many ways to move this valuable resource to where it is needed. This is called irrigation. Some methods include:

- River diversions.
- Dams and canals, such as those from 3100BC in Egypt.
- Tunnels – such as in Sri Lanka from 300BC.
- Shaduf – a bucket balanced on a beam, used in many countries from early times.
- Qanat – systems of wells and tunnels, used as early as 800BC in Iran.
- Archimedes screw – a cylinder with a large screw inside for pushing water upwards, used from 3rd century BC.

Even the simplest of these irrigation methods are still used in parts of the world: getting water to go where we want it, including by forcing it uphill, is one of the great human achievements!

Tractors

Heavy farm machinery was worked by animals such as oxen, and later, horses. Animals were slowly replaced by steam engines. Switching to a lighter gasoline-powered engine led to the first tractor in 1892, which was invented by John Froelich in Iowa, USA.

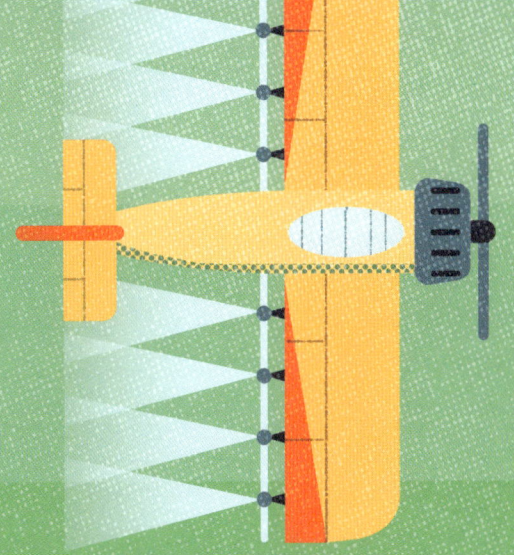

Growth booster

Another major advance was man-made fertiliser. Until 1913, farmers used animal dung and some minerals to keep the soil healthy. Then two German scientists, Fritz Haber and Carl Bosch, used nitrogen gas to make artificial fertiliser that helped crops grow better. This made farms much more productive, but nitrous oxide is a greenhouse gas, so it has also contributed to climate change.

TECHNOLOGY

FOOD THE RACE TO EAT BETTER

For thousands of years, people learned to keep food in good condition by using salt, spices, smoking it over a fire, pickling or drying it. Major advances in preserving food came in the 19th century.

Early meals

Some methods of preparing or preserving food have been around for as long as we can remember. For example, grinding grain into flour so we can bake bread, and fermenting foods so they last longer (such as turning milk into cheese). Other ancient advances include forging metal pots to cook food over a fire, and making knives to cut food.

Cool facts

Can you imagine life without a fridge? Many foods keep better in the cold. Ice was once so valuable that it was carved from lakes and transported round the world. This changed with the development of the refrigerator, which cools using compressed gas. The first one whirred into action in 1851, invented in America by John Gorrie. But it took the introduction of electric fridges, invented in 1913 by fellow American Fred W. Wolf, for their use to spread.

Canned food

The first canned food was made by Frenchman Nicolas Appert for the French military. People had been trying for years to either remove air from food or preserve it with heat. He did both in 1803, starting with sealed glass jars and switching to metal cans. Mind you, there was something missing: soldiers had to open the tins with hammers or bayonets until proper tin openers were invented in 1858!

Hot and cold

In 1924 Clarence Birdseye invented a freezing method similar to the one used today. Freeze drying (which freezes fast, without air) was first used during World War 2 (1939-1945) to send blood to treat wounded soldiers and is now used for foods.

The first microwave oven was sold in 1955. The machine was invented by Percy Spencer who was working with microwave radar when a chocolate bar near his equipment melted. He was the first person to investigate what was happening. Microwave ovens were the result.

Pasteurisation

Bad food killed unlucky people who ate or drank it for thousands of years because it carried invisible bacteria (germs). This happens a lot less today because of Louis Pasteur. In 1862 he showed that heating foods killed off dangerous bacteria in a process later named after him: pasteurisation. Milk, juices and many other foods are treated to make them safe to eat.

One to watch

Everybody needs water to live, but not everybody on the planet can get clean water all the time. This human achievement is on our 'to do' list. One in ten people don't have it close to home, while a quarter don't have a decent toilet of their own.

INDEX

aeroplanes 40, 56–57
Africa 34–35
Americas 26, 27
Amundsen, Roald 38–39
antibiotics 65
Armstrong, Neil 60, 61
astronomy 74–75, 77
Australia 36–37

bicycles 16–17, 50–51
black holes 77
Bolt, Usain 6, 13

cars 18–19, 48–49
China 24–25
Columbus, Christopher 26–27
communication 88–89
compasses 25, 47
computers 84–85
CT scans 71

Curie, Marie 72–73
cycling 16–17, 50–51

Darwin, Charles 66–67
diving 33
DNA 71

Earhart, Amelia 40–41
Einstein, Albert 77
electricity 49, 53, 80–81, 86, 87
entertainment 90–91
Everest 42–43
evolution 66–67
exploration 22–29, 32–39, 58–61

farming 92–93
first humans 34
flying 40–41, 56–57
food, preserving 94–95
Formula 1 18–19

gravity 76–77

Hillary, Edmund 42–43
hot-air balloons 54–55

Internet 85, 89

Livingstone, David 34–35

MacArthur, Ellen 30
Magellan, Ferdinand 28–29, 32
medicine 64–65, 68–71
Moon landings 58, 60–61
mountain climbing 42–43
MRI (magnetic resonance imaging) 71

Newton, Isaac 76–77

Olympic games 12–13

Paralympics 14–15
pasteurisation 95
Phelps, Michael 8, 13
Polo, Marco 24
postal system 25, 88
prosthetics 7, 15, 69

radiation 72–73
renewable energy 86–87
road systems 49
rockets 58–59
running races 6–7, 12, 13

sailing 26–31
satellites 58, 89
Scott, Robert 38–39
ships and boats 30, 31, 46–47
skating 13, 21
skiing 13, 15, 20–21
solar power 47, 57, 87

South Pole 38–39
space exploration 58–61
steam power 47, 52
swimming 8–9, 13, 15

televisions 89, 91
Tenzing Norgay 42–43
throwing sports 10–11
trains 52–53

ultrasound 70
undersea exploration 32–33

video games 91

wheels 15, 17, 18, 48, 50, 51, 82–83
Wright brothers 56
writing systems 88

X-rays 70

Quarto is the authority on a wide range of topics.
Quarto educates, entertains and enriches the lives of our readers—enthusiasts and lovers of hands-on living.
www.quartoknows.com

Editors: Harriet Stone and Ellie Brough
Designer: Mike Henson
Editorial Director: Rhiannon Findlay
Group Publisher: Maxime Boucknooghe

© 2020 Quarto Publishing plc

This edition first published in 2020 by QED Publishing, an imprint of The Quarto Group.
The Old Brewery, 6 Blundell Street,
London N7 9BH, United Kingdom.
T (0)20 7700 6700 F (0)20 7700 8066
www.QuartoKnows.com

All rights reserved. No part of this publication may be reproduced, stored in a retrieval system, or transmitted in any form or by any means, electronic, mechanical, photocopying, recording, or otherwise, without the prior permission of the publisher, nor be otherwise circulated in any form of binding or cover other than that in which it is published and without a similar condition being imposed on the subsequent purchaser.

A catalogue record for this book is available from the British Library.

ISBN 978 0 7112 5667 5

Manufactured in Guangdong, China CC072020

9 8 7 6 5 4 3 2 1

MIX
Paper from responsible sources
FSC www.fsc.org FSC C008047